"For traditional southern cooking . . . Atlantans love Mary Mac's—and loyally insist that if one hasn't eaten there, one hasn't begun to learn about food in their city. This . . . restaurant is touted by some as 'the only good food in town,' and we heard more than once that there's no hope of getting a table when the Georgia legislature is in session. . . . For unembellished southern cooking, Mary Mac's is the place."

—Mimi Elder, *Gourmet*

"Mary Mac's . . . food is a miracle of prodigious goodness."

—Bert Green, *Cuisine*

"Mary Mac's, a bastion of southern cooking . . . a homespun downtown Atlanta restaurant that attracts taxicab drivers and bank presidents . . . haven for people who crave down-home food that is simple and substantial in the findest tradition of Southern cooking."

—Bill Lohmann, UPI

"Mary Mac's specializes in the kind of southern food that unfortunately is disappearing: fried chicken—definitely the best anywhere—corn bread and pot likker—the juice left from cooking greens."

—*Esquire*

"Margaret Kennon Lupo threads her way through the multilevel mecca of southern cooking . . . the queen of cuisine, Dixie style."

—Alan Patureau, staff writer,
The Sunday Atlanta Journal & Constitution

"Mary Mac's means simply and without qualification the best home-cooked southern food you'll ever eat."

—Sara Spano, *The Sunday Ledger-Enquirer* (Columbus, Georgia)

SOUTHERN COOKING

FROM

Mary Mac's Tea Room

SOUTHERN COOKING

FROM

Mary Mac's Tea Room

REVISED, UPDATED, AND EXPANDED

By Margaret Lupo

A DELL TRADE PAPERBACK

Contents

About Mary Mac's Tea Room

Mary Mac's Tea Room is a relic from an era forty or so years ago, when Atlanta had a dozen or more tearooms. The story is that ladies who lost their husbands in the war turned to what they knew best—hospitality—to put food in their children's mouths. First that meant boardinghouses—when some were smart enough to realize it was easier, and made more money, to open dining rooms close to the business section. They called them "tearooms" to sound more genteel, or ladylike. Believe me, by the time I came along, they were all hardheaded businesswomen. When I bought Mary Mac's in 1962 from its founder, Mary McKenzie, it was a seventy-five-seat restaurant. Now we can seat over 350 and we serve an average of 2,000 meals each day!

Mary Mac's still has the world's best fried chicken, and lots of pork and seafood dishes as well as beef. We still pick over turnip greens and wash them by hand; still snap fresh green beans and cut fresh corn off the cob. We offer our own luscious hot breads baked in our own kitchens, and old-fashioned puddings for dessert. We are plain, not fancy, and so are our prices!

We are located in midtown, right on the edge of Atlanta's downtown business section. At lunch we serve businesspeople, bank presidents, politicians, college faculty members, taxi drivers (our best press agents), and so on. It is a remarkably cosmopolitan audience, and becomes even more so in the evenings. We're close to the famous Fox Theatre, the Civic Center, and the High Museum, so we get stars and chorus people as well as families. We've had to instruct our front people that VIPs come to eat, not to be approached for autographs.

And those are a whole lot of other stories—the prince and his beautiful princess, the man who stripped naked, the star who was nasty, and the star who was a doll—someday I'm going to write a book. . . .

We've received lots of wonderful praise over the years, and since we've worked hard to achieve it, I hope you won't think it immodest if I share some of it with you.

About This Book

The first edition of *Southern Cooking from Mary Mac's Tea Room* was published in 1982 and sold many, many copies in the Atlanta area. It got such a great reception from all my friends and strangers alike that I could hardly wait to write the new edition—to add the recipes we love to do at home as well as more of the ones we use at Mary Mac's. Some of my friends have contributed recipes for food I have enjoyed at their homes—my siblings and children are all enthusiastic cooks and their favorites are also contained herein.

All recipes are easy to follow—they are set up in the style in which we train cooks at the Tea Room. Step by step, first do this and then do that—it is an easy way to approach a new recipe.

Measures

A few grains, pinch (dry) = Less than ⅛ teaspoon

Dash (liquid) = 2 or 3 drops

1 tablespoon = 3 teaspoons

1 fluid ounce = 2 tablespoons = ⅛ cup

¼ cup = 4 tablespoons = 2 fluid ounces

⅓ cup = 5⅓ tablespoons = 2⅔ fluid ounces

½ cup = 8 tablespoons = 4 fluid ounces

¾ cup = 12 tablespoons = 6 fluid ounces

1 cup = 16 tablespoons = 8 fluid ounces

1 cup (liquid) = ½ pint

1 pint = 2 cups (liquid) = 16 fluid ounces

1 quart = 2 pints = 32 fluid ounces

1 gallon = 4 quarts

1 pound (dry) = 16 ounces

¼-pound stick butter = ½ cup

Definitions

Braise. To brown slowly in fat, then add liquid, cover pan, and simmer on top of stove or bake in oven.

Chives. An herb with a delicate onion flavor similar to tops of small early spring onions.

Collards. Large-leafed southern greens at their peak in the spring and fall; tougher than turnip greens and generally cooked wiith salt pork.

Crackermeal. Fine meal (finer than cornmeal) made from crackers and used as a more delicate coating for meats. Available in grocery stores or can be made by rolling unsalted soda crackers on a wooden board with a rolling pin.

Cream. To rub or stir together with a spoon to make texture soft, creamy, and smooth.

Crimp. To seal pastry by trimming edges of pastry to cover edges of baking dish and pressing bottom of fork tines along edge of dish, sealing pastry.

Deep-fry. To cook in hot oil or fat that is deep enough to cover the food completely.

Devein. Commonly refers to cleaning the small black filament from the back of a shrimp or pawn either before or after cooking.

Dredge. To coat all over with flour or other dry mixture.

Drippings. The melted fat from bacon or fatback. Strain through fine mesh and refrigerate to use for seasoning.

Dutch Oven. A heavy saucepan with a tight heavy lid.

Fatback. Pure pork fat cut from the back of the pig, fresh or cured in salt.

Filé Powder. A fine powder made of dried sassafras leaves and other herbs, used especially in gumbo. Available in gourmet shops.

Fillet. To cut cleaned, deheaded, and scaled fish down both sides of the backbone into two lean boneless pieces. Also the name of the pieces thus cut.

Flour, All-purpose. Also known as *plain flour*; contains only flour, no salt or baking powder.

Fold. To gently incorporate one foodstuff into another without breaking it, particularly egg white, which needs to remain fluffy.

Garlic Clove. One bud from the whole garlic bulb or cluster.

Glaze. Melted butter, milk, or other ingredient brushed on top of a food to make it shiny or glossy.

Grits. A favorite side dish for a southern breakfast and any meal. Grits are the broken grains for corn hominy, which is corn with the hull and germ removed. Grits are served (hot) with butter or gravy.

Julienne. To cut into matchstick strips about 2 inches by ⅛ inch.

Kitchen Bouquet. A vegetable-based browning and seasoning sauce.

Knead. To fold dough and press with the heel of your hand until it is smooth and elastic.

Marinate. To soak food in a highly seasoned liquid to impart flavor as well as to tenderize.

Muscadine. An old-fashioned country grape often grown on a backyard arbor in combination with scuppernongs. Both grapes are small, thumbnail size, the scuppernong a brown-skinned fruit from which a light-colored jelly can be made, the muscadine, a heavier, redder fruit, almost purple, which will make dark-red flavorful jelly often used in the South with fresh game. Melted jelly makes a good dessert sauce with ice cream or pound cake.

Pepper. *Black pepper:* crushed from underripe sundried while berries; *most* universally used seasoning.

 Cayenne pepper: finely ground, very, very hot; does not retain flavor as well as red pepper flakes.

 Peppercorns: dried kernels of the pepper berries, black, white, or green. Especially good to use on salads, freshly ground in a peppermill.

 Red pepper: coarse dried flakes of pungent hot red peppers. Retains flavor much longer than cayenne and is easy to measure by the "pinch."

 White pepper: made from fully ripe berries, the dark outer coat having been buffed off. Good to use with whipped potatoes, cream sauces, light-colored gravies, vegetables, and soufflés.

Pepper Vinegar. A bottled sauce made from small red and green peppers steeped in vinegar. Used on turnip greens, in soups, on smoked oysters or clams.

Pot Likker. See recipe, p. 20.

Reseason. To use a little more of seasonings you started with to restore any flavor lost in cooking.

Roux. A mixture of equal parts butter, or other fats, and flour cooked together for use as a thickening agent in sauces and gravies.

Rutabagas. A deep yellow turnip.

Salt Pork. Generally pork fat cured in salt.

Sauté. To stir lightly in an open pan in a small amount of very hot margarine or butter and oil to brown evenly and seal in juices.

Scallions. Twin sister of green onion, a term often used interchangeably. Usually a bit larger than green onion; about the size of a finger.

Simmer. To cook food in water or other liquid that is bubbling gently.

Spring onions, or, **green onions.** A term used to describe long, slim onions the size of a pencil with green tops and slightly bulbous bottoms. Spring onion is the old-fashioned term—we used to have them only in the spring, when home gardens produced them.

Steam. To cook food with a small amount of boiling water in a tightly covered pot.

Tabasco Sauce. A bottled juice made from red peppers, used lightly to enhance flavors or heavily in hot dishes.

Turmeric. An orange-colored spice, the chief ingredient of curry powder, used in salads and relishes and good with lamb.

Whisk. A wire whipping or beating utensil.

Hints from Mary Mac's

Making Gravies and Sauces

To make gravy and sauce from drippings, butter, margarine, or fat, use flour. To add richness to gravy and eliminate the floury taste, cook flour in drippings for 5 minutes *without browning* flour before adding stock or liquid.

To make gravy or sauce from a stock that has both fat and broth, use dissolved cornstarch instead of flour. Flour would become lumpy; cornstarch should be mixed with an equal amount of water in a separate bowl and then stirred or whipped into base stock for thickening.

In cream gravies, if calories are a concern, use milk instead of cream.

Gravies and sauces become smooth by stirring or beating continuously.

Storing Stocks and Drippings

To collect fat from soup or stock, cool soup or broth to room temperature and then place in refrigerator to allow fat to collect on top for easy removal and a clearer broth.

To store chicken fat collected from stock, melt fat down if it is hard, put in small containers, and place in refrigerator to use within 2 weeks or store in freezer for future use.

Freeze meat juices, stocks, and broths in small containers or in ice cube trays for future use. After stocks have been frozen in ice cube trays, remove cubes and place in sealed plastic bag to store.

Strain bacon drippings and save for future use in flavoring or frying. Bacon drippings can be stored at room temperature for 1 week or in the refrigerator indefinitely.

Frying

When deep-frying, oil or shortening should be hot, at least 350°. Fry food quickly to golden brown for a crisp crust and a juicy inside.

Always shake off excess coating mixture when preparing food for frying.

When deep-frying, do not overcrowd oil or shortening with food; overcrowding lowers temperature of the oil, and food may stick together.

To clear used frying oil or shortening, deep-fry potatoes in the used oil. Potatoes absorb the foreign ingredients and restore the oil to its original clarity for reuse in frying. Strain cleared oil, and store in covered container in refrigerator for future use. It keeps indefinitely.

Pastries

For flakier and more tender pastry, handle dough lightly and use as little additional flour on board and hands as possible. Use a minimum of liquid in dough to keep pastry from becoming too soft.

Roll out pastry quickly, then place rolled-out dough over filled dish. Press dough down inside baking dish to eliminate air between filling and pastry. Be sure pastry extends over edges of pan, then trim pastry with a sharp knife along edges of baking dish. Dip tines of fork in ice water, then press tines along edge of dish, sealing pastry. Fork tines make an attractive design. Always cut vent holes on top crust to allow steam to escape. An attractively cut pattern adds to the presentation of the dish.

Seafood

Never overcook shrimp. It is tastier when undercooked and will toughen when overcooked. See directions, page 105.

Serve fresh mountain trout with heads on for a traditional presentation.

To keep raw seafood fresh overnight, cover fish with ice and place in covered container in the refrigerator.

In our Atlanta supermarkets, those which have seafood departments always carry (on ice, of course) cans of pasteurized crabmeat, clams, and oysters. These are fresh, have been lightly steamed and are just as good (well, almost) as fresh. The canned type of seafood which does not have to be refrigerated does not do well in these recipes.

Vegetables

To save time, slice celery in the bunch, holding it down on a cutting board and slicing diagonally to eliminate strings. Then wash chopped celery in a colander.

When baking vegetables, other than in soufflés, line baking pan with aluminum foil for easier cleaning.

Use as little water as possible to steam vegetables as the water used will absorb the flavor of the vegetable. Any leftover vegetable broth provides a good stock for use in making sauces or vegetable soup.

Seasoning

Chicken broth may be used as a substitute for, or in addition to, bacon drippings or salt pork to season vegetables. The flavor is mild, has fewer calories, and increases the flavor of the vegetable.

Flavors are enhanced when meat and seafood are cooked with the bones in.

If soup or stew is slightly scorched, pour soup out of pot into a clean pot and stir in 1 teaspoon of mustard to eliminate the scorched flavor.

Use salt sparingly. It can always be added but never taken away.

Use ground white pepper (preferably freshly ground) for a mild pepper seasoning, as it is not as strong as black pepper.

Try different seasonings in a bland cream sauce, one at a time (garlic, celery, herbs, etc.), until you determine what appeals to your family. This also educates your own taste buds as to exactly what flavor you want to add to a certain dish.

Pasta

To keep cooked noodles or pasta from sticking, add 1 teaspoon of vegetable oil to water in which noodles will be cooked or stir a small amount of oil into cooked and drained noodles.

Appetizers

Catfish and Caviar • Marinated Mushrooms • Stuffed Mush-
rooms • Nacho Supreme Dip • San Diego Salsa • Salsa
Fresca • Hot Bloody Mary • Pork, Peaches, and Peanuts Dip
• Crabmeat Spread • Chicken Liver Pâté • Spinach Dip •
Spiced Shrimp • Shrimp Cocktail • Roasted Salted Pecans •
Spiced Peanuts

Whichever term you use for food to serve with drinks or at the
beginning of a meal—appetizers, starters, or hors d'oeuvres—
the food itself should be light and easy (and fun) so the cook
doesn't get stuck in the kitchen instead of with the guests or
family. These recipes can be used for party fare, home fare, or
snacks.

Most of my soups are main courses—another chapter entirely.

Catfish and Caviar

Serves party of 15 to 20 people as one of several dishes.

I invented this recipe when I had leftover catfish and needed a dish to take to a neighborhood party.

Clean and bake in 350° oven:

> 1   **12- to 14-ounce whole catfish** *or* **2 6-ounce catfish fillets**

Remove any black skin and all bones.

Mix together:

> 1   **cup sour cream**
> 3   **spring onions, chopped fine**
> ⅓   **teaspoon Worcestershire sauce**
>   **several dashes Tabasco sauce**

Add the catfish, flaked into ½-inch pieces.

Spread in shallow dish and top with:

> **3½ ounces black caviar.***

This dip is best with toasted bagel rings.

---

*Romanoff Black Lumpfish is my favorite medium-priced caviar.

Marinated Mushrooms

I marinate any mushrooms left over from salad or soup making—they keep well that way about one week and can be used in many ways.

Rinse and pat dry:

mushrooms

Cut to a size easy to lift on toothpick.

Cover with a good clear Italian dressing* or with half red wine and half soy sauce. Marinate in refrigerator overnight.

Good as an hors d'oeuvre or as a part of a make-your-own salad, or as a garnish around roast beef.

*I've never found a French, Thousand Island, or blue cheese salad dressing I like better than my own—but Italian I have. Find one you like—it's a time saver.

Stuffed Mushrooms

YIELD: ONE TEN-INCH PLATTER OF HORS D'OEUVRES

Remove and reserve stems and rinse:

1   **pound medium-sized fresh mushrooms**

Bring to boil:

1   **quart water**
1   **teaspoon salt**
½   **lemon, chopped**

Drop in mushroom caps, bring back to boil, and remove from heat. Leave mushrooms in water for 5 minutes. Drain well, reserving liquid.

Meanwhile, chop stems fine.

Melt in heavy pan:

½   **stick butter**

Add the chopped mushroom stems and:

4   **garlic cloves, minced**
½   **cup finely chopped pecan pieces**

Sauté lightly for 3 or 4 minutes.

Cool and add:

1   **cup chopped fresh parsley**
½   **cup toasted fine bread crumbs**
2   **teaspoons reserved cooking liquid, if mixture seems too dry**

Stuff the mushroom caps with the pecan mixture. Serve at room temperature or heat in buttered dish in 400° oven for 5 minutes.

Nacho Supreme Dip

A masterpiece from Atlanta West, my daughter Barbara's restaurant in San Diego, where fresh jalapeños are easily available and where people love hot flavors. Barbara uses fresh peppers, seeded and chopped. Do remember to wash your hands thoroughly after handling!

Cook and drain:

> ½ pound ground beef

Warm slightly:

> 2 cups canned refried beans

In a 12 × 8 × 2-inch (or longer) serving dish, layer the beef, then the beans, then add a layer of each of the following:

> 2 cups chopped fresh tomato
> 2 cups grated Jack cheese
> 2 cups sliced ripe (black) olives
> 1 cup chopped scallion
> 2 cups diced peeled ripe avocado
> ½ cup sliced fresh jalapeños

Spread dish with:

> ½ inch sour cream

Serve with crisp corn or flour tortilla chips for dipping.

San Diego Salsa

Another terrific dish from Atlanta West. If you and yours have ever had a Mexican food craze, you know salsa is a prime ingredient for delicious taste. This recipe and the one that follows give you either a salsa to hold in your refrigerator for the next week or a fresh one to use today.

Combine in heavy pot:

1	16-ounce can whole tomatoes, crushed
2	bunches scallions, chopped
½	cup sliced fresh jalapeños
¼	cup white vinegar
	garlic salt to taste *or* 1 garlic clove, minced

Simmer for 15 minutes. The salsa will keep, refrigerated, for 3 weeks.

Serve with corn or taco chips or with any Mexican main dish.

Salsa Fresca

Prepare San Diego Salsa, substituting for the can of tomatoes chopped peeled fresh tomatoes:

Do *not* heat!

Add:

1	bunch cilantro, chopped

Hot Bloody Mary

HOT BLOODY MARY MAKES 2 QUARTS.
WILL FILL ABOUT 20 MUGS.

Bring to boil:

> 2   cups beef stock (page 16)

Add:

> 1   cup minced celery
> ½   cup minced green bell pepper
> 1   28-ounce can tomatoes, chopped fine*

Simmer for about 5 minutes, then add:

> 3   12-ounce cans tomato juice
>   several dashes Tabasco sauce
>   several dashes Worcestershire sauce
> ½   teaspoon garlic salt

Taste. Add salt and freshly ground pepper if necessary.

Warm mixture and pour into heatproof pitcher. Place one ounce vodka and one slice lemon in each mug; pour mixture over and serve at once. A .750 liter of vodka will suffice.

---

*Be sure the tomatoes are in small enough pieces for your guests to swallow.

Pork, Peaches, and Peanuts Dip

YIELD: SIX CUPS

Cut into 1-inch cubes:

    4   pounds boneless lean pork

Mix:

    1   cup soy sauce
    1   cup red wine vinegar
    3   garlic cloves, chopped

Add pork to marinade and leave at room temperature for 1 hour or cover and refrigerate overnight. Preheat oven to 300°.

Place in 3-quart ovenproof casserole and add:

    2   cups water

Cover and bake for 2 hours.

Remove meat; cool meat and drippings separately. Chop pork. To get the right texture, do this by hand. It should not be too fine.

Add:

    1   cup cooled, skimmed pan drippings
    1   cup hot sweet mustard
    1   cup peach conserve or peeled fresh chopped peaches
        (*not* jelly or preserves)
    1   pinch hot red pepper flakes

Mixture should spread easily.

Coarsely chop:

    ½   pound salted roasted peanuts

Mix into the pork mixture if you plan to use it immediately, or use the peanuts to garnish the dip.

This is dark and spicy, so use toasted plain bagel rings or any plain crackers.

Crabmeat Spread

YIELD: 2½ CUPS

Pick over and remove any shells from:

    12 ounces fresh crabmeat or 12-ounce can pasteurized
        crabmeat from your seafood counter (do not resteam)

Combine in bowl:

    3   ribs celery, chopped fine
    2   tablespoons finely chopped fresh parsley
    ½   cup mayonnaise (page 194)
        juice of 1 lemon
    1   teaspoon good-quality hot (not sweet) mustard
    ½   cup cream

Mix well, add crabmeat, and taste for salt and freshly ground white pepper. Serve with your choice of plain or whole wheat crackers.

Chicken Liver Pâté

Melt:

½   stick margarine or butter

Add:

1   pound rinsed, drained chicken livers
¼   cup finely chopped green onion

Sauté for 4 or 5 minutes and remove from heat.

If livers are still too rare for your taste, return to heat for another couple of minutes, stirring constantly. Mash with fork or blender.

Let cool to room temperature, then add:

2   tablespoons dry white wine
¼   cup heavy cream
    several dashes Tabasco sauce
    salt and freshly ground white pepper to taste

Serve with crusty French bread hand-broken into small chunks.

Spinach Dip

YIELD: 2 CUPS

Thaw out and drain well:

1   10-ounce package chopped spinach

Squeeze to remove excess liquid. Pat dry with paper towels.

Stir into the spinach:

> 1½ tablespoons lemon juice
> ⅓ cup chopped scallion
> ½ cup sour cream
> ½ cup mayonnaise (page 194)
> ½ teaspoon dried oregano
> ½ teaspoon dried dill

This recipe may easily be doubled or tripled for party use. It retains color and flavor well overnight in the refrigerator. Serve with crisp crackers.

Spiced Shrimp

Cook, cool, and peel shrimp as for shrimp cocktail (page 12).

Place in refrigerator bowl with tight lid:

> 1 medium onion, sliced thin
> 1 medium red or yellow bell pepper, sliced thin
> 1 teaspoon pickling spice
> 1 teaspoon fresh or dried dill
> ½ teaspoon hot red pepper flakes
> 1 cup vinegar
> ½ cup water
> 1½ cups vegetable oil
> ½ cup dry white wine

Mix well and add shrimp. Cover tightly and refrigerate overnight.

Serve these tasty shrimp on toothpicks; offer crackers if you wish.

Shrimp Cocktail

ONE POUND OF SHRIMP SHOULD SERVE 3 PEOPLE

One of my husband's favorite things was boiled shrimp with a cold sauce hot enough to burn your tonsils.

Bring to boil:

1	**quart water**
1	**tablespoon salt**
½	**lemon, cut into pieces**

Pour shrimp into the boiling water. *

Bring back to boil and remove from heat. Leave shrimp in water for 3 minutes. Remove from hot water and immediately run cold water over the shrimp.

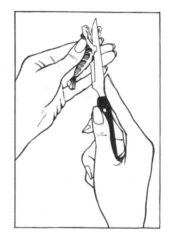

To shell the shrimp, hold it just below the fantail; break the shell off at this point in order to keep the tail whole. Pull the shell off and cut shrimp very slightly down the back in order to remove the sand vein. Serve with seafood sauce (page 214).

---

*Small shrimp are too much trouble to clean and do not have the lobsterlike texture of larger shrimp. Allow at least 4 large shrimp per person.

Roasted Salted Pecans

YIELD: 3½ TO 4 CUPS

Place in heavy baking pan:

  ¼ **cup melted butter**
  4   **cups pecan halves**

Bake in a 250° oven 30 minutes. Remove, stir well, and return to oven for about another 10 minutes. Sprinkle with salt, allow to cool, store in glass jar with tight lid. Try garlic salt for an entirely different taste.

Spiced Peanuts

YIELD: 4 CUPS

Place in heavy baking pan:

  ½ **cup melted butter**
  4   **cups whole Spanish peanuts**
  ½ **teaspoon garlic salt**
  ½ **teaspoon curry powder**

Bake at 250° for 15 minutes, until thoroughly hot. Remove from oven, cool, and use or store in glass jar with tight lid.

Both of these recipes will store about one week unrefrigerated or one month refrigerated. I've never had them last long if any young ones are around. . . .

Soups and Stocks

Beef Stock • Chicken Stock • Shrimp Stock • Southern Vegetable Soup • Pot Likker • Chicken Soup • Cajun Soup • Marie's Chicken and Vegetable Soup • Seafood Chowder • Clear Fish Soup • Onion Soup • Seafood Gumbo • Paul's Seafood Gumbo • Austin Ford's Gumbo • Oyster Stew • Leek and Potato Soup with Crabmeat • Broccoli or Cauliflower Soup • Black Bean Soup

Soup is good food, as the radio and TV keep telling us. However, it is so easy and so inexpensive to make soup from scratch (most of the time) that I love to make it myself. Almost anything goes, although I must admit I don't really care for sweet soups. Most of my soups are main dishes or can be used as such. Add more broth if you want a lighter soup, and do investigate all your leftovers before you choose which soup to make.

Boil the bones and strain the broth—then be creative.

Beef Stock

Good *flavorful beef stock is made from beef bones. Starting with cold water draws the juices for the stock.*

Rinse under cold running water:

> 2 beef bones *or* 1 soup bone with lots of marrow (about 2 pounds)

Place them in a large pot and add:

> 3 quarts cold water
> 2 teaspoons salt
>   celery tops
> ½ large onion

Bring to a boil, reduce to simmer, and partially cover. Simmer for 1½ to 2 hours. Strain before using.

If not for immediate use, cool, skim off fat, and keep, covered and refrigerated, about 2 weeks; or freeze in ice cube trays, place cubes in sealed plastic bag, and place in freezer for up to several months.

Chicken Stock

Remove giblets, * *clean cavity out well under running water, and rinse:*

1   **5- to 6-pound hen**

Cut the hen apart if you wish—it will cook more quickly—but use all the bones.

Place in stockpot and add:

3   **quarts water (or enough to cover)**
2   **teaspoons salt**
    celery pieces or leaves (optional)
    a few slices onion (optional)

Bring to a boil, reduce to simmer, and simmer covered, about 2 hours. Remove chicken from stock. Remove chicken meat from bones for use in chicken soup (page 21), chicken pan pie (page 62), or other chicken dishes.

Strain stock. If you do not need the stock immediately, cool, skim off fat, and freeze in ice cube trays or small freezer containers. After freezing, transfer to sealed plastic bags. The stock will keep for several months in freezer. It can be used in soups, sauces, and gravies.

---

*I don't think giblets make a good, clear chicken stock, but they do freeze well. Save them if you wish, for use, chopped, in chicken gravy.

Shrimp Stock

Wash:

> 1   **pound shrimp**

Bring to boil in 2-quart saucepan:

> 4   **cups water**

Add:

> ½   **lemon, sliced**
> ½   **teaspoon salt**

Add shrimp to boiling water. Bring back to boil. Then immediately pour shrimp into colander with pan underneath to catch shrimp stock. Set stock aside to cool. Cool shrimp with crushed ice or under cold running water. Use shrimp for any seafood dish.

If stock is not to be used immediately, cool, pour into ice cube trays, and freeze into cubes. Store in sealed plastic bags in freezer for use in seafood dishes.

This makes a mild base for Creole sauce (page 208) or almost any fairly liquid seafood sauce. For a stronger flavor, return shrimp shells to stock and cook until liquid is reduced by half.

Southern Vegetable Soup

MAKES 2 TO 3 QUARTS

Place in heavy 3-quart pot:

1   medium onion, chopped
4   cups chicken stock (page 17)
1   28-ounce can crushed tomatoes, with juice
1   cup beef stock (page 16)
1   cup chopped cooked chicken, beef, or pork

Bring this base to a boil and simmer, covered, 30 minutes. Add salt and freshly ground white pepper to taste.

Now add any leftover cooked vegetables you have—corn, rice, potatoes, peas—and of course you may use any raw vegetables you wish (but be sure to add the cooked vegetables last). They need to be chopped small, and they may make your soup broth cloudy, but there's nothing wrong with that—it's all a matter of taste.

If you have no leftovers (can it be?), use small cans of corn and green peas. Rinse them off before you drop them into the soup stock. One baking potato cut into cubes should be boiled separately for 5 minutes before adding it.

Southern vegetable soup must have okra in it—either drop in frozen okra at the last moment or slice a few pods of fresh okra, which will cook almost as quickly.

Sweet vegetables such as carrots have a special tang and are a matter of personal preference.

Add salt, freshly ground pepper, and a dash of Tabasco, and you're all ready. With some crisp crackers or some hot cornbread, you have a meal.

Pot Likker

You must have turnip greens for this, of course—see the recipe for turnip greens in Chapter 6.

Cube:

   1   **ounce fatback***

Fry cubes slowly in heavy frying pan until they are brown, being careful not to burn the drippings.

Place in a 3-quart pot:

   2   **cups chicken stock (page 17)**
   2   **cups water (or chicken broth for a richer soup)**
        the cooked fatback cubes and drippings (optional)
   1   **cup cooked turnip greens and juice (page 168)**

Simmer for at least 5 minutes. Taste and season with salt, freshly ground white pepper, and a dash of Tabasco sauce or pepper vinegar.

Serve hot, with hot hoecakes (page 232) to crumble into your bowl.

---

*If your taste—or your doctor—says no fatback or pork drippings, leave it out. Add more chicken broth and proceed as above. But don't forget the cornbread!

Chicken Soup

Chicken soup is so simple—and so good—and has so many variations that a recipe seems almost unnecessary. Your love of good food and your imagination are all that are really required. Start with a 4 or 5 pound hen, with not too much fat, since the need for all that richness and calories is long gone.

Place in heavy pot with tight lid:

6   **cups chicken stock (page 17)**
½   **cup finely chopped onion**
½   **cup chopped celery**

Bring to boil, reduce to simmer, and simmer, covered, for 5 minutes.

Add:

1   **cup cooked rice, noodles, potatoes, or a combination**
1   **cup chopped cooked chicken**
½   **teaspoon salt**
¼   **teaspoon freshly ground pepper**

Before the last 5 minutes of simmering add chopped fresh parsley, green peas, sliced okra, or whatever you like—have fun!

Bring back to boil, reduce to simmer, and simmer for another 5 minutes. Taste and reseason.

Cajun Soup

Place in heavy pot with tight lid:

1½	pounds chicken (6 thighs do well)
6	cups water
1	tablespoon salt
2	ounces smoked sausage, sliced thin

Simmer for 1 hour, then add:

1	cup chopped celery
½	cup chopped onion
6	scallions, chopped
2	garlic cloves, chopped
1	tablespoon chopped fresh parsley
1	teaspoon salt
½	teaspoon freshly ground white pepper
2	dashes Tabasco sauce
1	dash hot red pepper flakes
1	10-ounce can RoTel tomatoes and green chilies*
1	14-ounce can tomatoes, chopped, with juice

Simmer about 30 minutes more, then add:

1	cup cooked rice (more if you like the soup thicker)

Taste. If soup is too hot for your family's taste, add water and simmer awhile longer.

Cool and store in refrigerator. It is much better the second day, if you can bear to wait. Bone the chicken thighs, chop the meat, and add it, if you wish.

---

*Do try the RoTel tomatoes and green chilies, if you never have. They're good in chili and almost any Cajun dish calling for tomatoes.

Marie's Chicken and Vegetable Soup

Marie, number four daughter, is a good cook and loves to cook, as all my children do.

Bring to boil:

    2   quarts chicken stock (page 17)

Add:

    5   tablespoons chopped scallion
    1   red pepper, chopped
        kernels cut from 2 ears corn
    2   tablespoons chopped celery
    1   teaspoon chopped fresh rosemary
    ½   teaspoon freshly ground pepper
    1   teaspoon salt

Simmer for 15 to 30 minutes and add:

    2   boned raw whole chicken breasts, chopped
    2   tablespoons chopped fresh parsley

Simmer until chicken is done, about 10 minutes.

Seafood Chowder

MAKES 2 QUARTS

Melt in heavy 3-quart pot:

2 tablespoons strained bacon drippings

Add:

2 tablespoons all-purpose flour

Mix well and cook over very low heat (do not brown) for 5 minutes.
Then add, stirring constantly:

2 cups shrimp stock (page 18)
2 cups chicken stock (page 17)
1 teaspoon salt
½ teaspoon freshly ground white pepper

When the broth or stock is thick and clear, add:

2 cups peeled, cubed potato
½ cup chopped celery
½ cup chopped white onion
½ cup chopped scallion
1 garlic clove, chopped

Cover tightly to steam for about 5 minutes.

Add:

1 cup heavy cream*
2 cups cooked seafood—scallops, chopped clams,
   crabmeat, shrimp, or whatever you like

Bring back to boil and simmer gently 2 minutes to "marry" all flavors.
This is an easy way to make chowder.

_____

*You may substitute milk for the cream or just use water, if you wish a lighter,
less caloric soup—but chowder indicates potoates and a pork flavor.

Clear Fish Soup

This is a clear, unthickened soup, easy to make and delicious.

Bring to a boil in a gallon pot:

    2   quarts water
    1   tablespoon salt

Add:

    ½   pound shrimp, rinsed
    ½   pound bay scallops
    ½   pound white flaky fish

Bring back to boil and remove from heat. With slotted spoon, remove seafood. Peel and devein shrimp. Slice each shrimp lengthwise. Skim or strain broth and bring back to boil.

Add:

    1   garlic clove, minced
    2   tablespoons chopped chives or scallion
    ½   cup fresh savory, washed and chopped

Simmer for 10 minutes, then add:

    1   cup sliced fresh mushrooms
    1   cup sliced cooked new potatoes (skin on)
    1   cup broccoli flowerets
    1   tablespoon butter

Lastly, add the seafood.

Bring to boil and serve or set aside to cool and refrigerate, covered, up to 2 days.

Onion Soup

Melt in heavy frying pan:

> 1   tablespoon butter

Add:

> 1   tablespoon vegetable oil
> 1   garlic clove, minced
> 4   medium white onions, sliced thin

Stir constantly until onions are lightly browned. Lift them aside.

Add:

> 2   tablespoons all-purpose flour

Stir until flour is absorbed into the butter-oil. Let this roux cook very slowly for 5 minutes, being careful not to burn it.

Bring to simmer in gallon Dutch oven:

> 3   cups beef stock (page 16) or canned beef consommé
> 1   cup water
> 1   teaspoon salt
> ½   teaspoon freshly ground black pepper
>   dash of Tabasco sauce

Add roux, stirring constantly to keep smooth. Taste and reseason. Add cooked onions.

Place a round of toasted French bread in each of four ovenproof bowls; pour soup over them, top with freshly grated Parmesan cheese, and put them under hot broiler until cheese is browned. Serve immediately—and carefully!—with more toasted French bread.

Seafood Gumbo

"Gumbo" is a deep south term meaning a thick stew made with lots of okra, tomatoes, and filé powder. This is a seafood gumbo, but chicken would do well too.

Heat in large Dutch oven:

2	cups shrimp stock (page 18)
2	cups chicken stock (page 17)
½	cup chopped white onion
½	cup chopped leek or chives
1	12-ounce can tomatoes, chopped, with juice
½	small dried red pepper
1	large garlic clove, minced
2	tablespoons butter

Simmer gently until onion is soft, about 10 minutes. Remove red pepper.

Season gumbo with:

salt and freshly ground white pepper to taste
Tabasco sauce to taste
a few drops Kitchen Bouquet (to color the broth a light brown)

Add:

1	cup trimmed and sliced fresh okra, ¼ inch thick
3	cups cooked seafood—lobster, crabmeat, scallops, any mild white fish in chunks, shrimp, etc.

Simmer very gently for 10 to 15 minutes, until okra is tender.

Just before serving, add:

2	tablespoons gumbo filé powder

Serve in soup bowls over rice.

Paul's Seafood Gumbo

MAKES 3 QUARTS

My brother, Paul Kennon, lives in Florida and is retired. He's a good cook, and his wife is smart enough to encourage him.

Melt in large heavy pot:

2 tablespoons shortening

Add:

2 tablespoons all-purpose flour

Cook over low heat, stirring constantly, until mixture is a deep rich brown.

Add:

2	quarts chicken stock (page 17)
½	cup chopped onion
½	cup chopped green bell pepper
½	cup chopped celery
1	large garlic clove, chopped fine

Bring to boil, reduce to simmer, and add:

1	tablespoon fresh lemon juice
1	tablespoon Worcestershire sauce
1	teaspoon Tabasco sauce
1	16-ounce can tomatoes, crushed
1	tablespoon dried parsley
1	teaspoon dried thyme
6½	ounces crabmeat (see note page xviii)
6½	ounces shucked clams
1	pound white flaky fish, chopped

Simmer for 1 hour and add:

1   pound fresh okra, washed, trimmed, and sliced into
½-inch pieces

½   pound large shrimp, cleaned, shelled, deveined, and
halved lengthwise

Simmer for 15 minutes more. Taste for salt and Tabasco sauce. Serve over rice.

Austin Ford's Gumbo

Father Ford, who set up a community center on the southwest side of Atlanta to help disadvantaged people in that neighborhood, is well known for his desire to feed the hungry, but not everybody knows what a good cook he is. Thank you, Father Ford! Prepare to spend your afternoon (day?) in the kitchen, however.

Cook together in heavy cast-iron skillet:

- 1½ cups vegetable oil
- 1½ cups all-purpose flour

Transfer to 2-gallon pot and add:

4	cups chopped onion
1	cup chopped green bell pepper
½	cup chopped scallion
½	cup chopped fresh parsley
2	teaspoons minced garlic
1	16-ounce can tomatoes, with juice
1	8-inch piece Polish or Andouille sausage, sliced
4	thin smoked pork chops, cubed
⅛	teaspoon each ground allspice, cloves, mace, coriander, and cardamom
3	teaspoons freshly ground black pepper
2	tablespoons salt
1	teaspoon cayenne pepper
	juice of 2 lemons
1	gallon water
4	pounds fresh okra, sliced

Simmer for 1 hour then add:

2	pounds peeled and deveined shrimp
½	pound crabmeat

Serve over rice. This is so rich that nothing else is needed—maybe a salad or a dessert. It makes a large amount—enough for 10 people to have plenty—but it does not divide easily to make less. Don't worry—if your guests don't eat it all, you will eat it happily tomorrow.

Oyster Stew

MAKES 5 SERVINGS

One of my husband's favorite dishes—only fresh oysters will do!

Drain over bowl:

1   pint shucked fresh oysters

Reserve liquid and set aside.

Melt in heavy 2-quart saucepan:

½   cup butter

When butter is bubbling, add drained oysters. Cook and stir over low heat for about 10 minutes, until oysters are well done.

Add the drained liquid from oysters and:

1   quart milk
1   pint cream
1   teaspoon salt
½   teaspoon freshly ground white pepper
½   teaspoon Worcestershire sauce
several dashes Tabasco sauce

Taste and reseason.

Sprinkle lightly with paprika, if you wish, and serve with small round oyster crackers, dropping several in each bowl as a garnish just before serving.

Leek and Potato Soup with Crabmeat

MAKES ABOUT 15 CUPS

I cannot resist giving you this country version of vichyssoise with crabmeat. When I invite a friend to my house for dinner, the first question usually is "Are we going to have crabmeat soup?"

Bring to boil in heavy Dutch oven:

5	cups chicken stock (page 17) or canned chicken broth
6	tablespoons butter
1	teaspoon salt
½	teaspoon freshly ground white pepper
2	dashes Tabasco sauce
2	dashes Worcestershire sauce

Add:

1	bunch (about 12 ounces) well-washed fresh leeks (*all but browned leaves*), chopped
1	bunch scallions, chopped
2	large garlic cloves, minced fine

Simmer for 30 minutes and add:

3	large Idaho potatoes (about 1½ pounds), peeled and diced

Simmer for another 30 minutes. Mash potatoes and onion mixture in the stock thoroughly with a potato masher.

Add:

4	cups milk
2	cups heavy cream

Taste and reseason. This should be a thick, heavy, creamy soup. If too thick, thin with milk and taste for seasonings.

Add:

2   cups cooked crabmeat, shrimp, or scallops*

Simmer soup for 5 minutes, and you have my favorite meal.

To steam crabs, place in pot with 2 inches of boiling water, 1 teaspoon of vinegar, and 2 teaspoons of salt. Cover and steam on high heat for approximately 30 minutes. Cool crab under cold tap water. Pick crab and drop crabmeat into soup.

If you use shrimp or scallops, sauté them quickly in butter, then add to the soup.

---

*My favorite addition is crabmeat. Steam live crabs and pick the meat from them or use pasteurized or frozen crab as a last resort. No canned seafood, please! The soup would be better with no seafood at all than with canned seafood.

Broccoli or Cauliflower Soup

MAKES 4 CUPS

This is a rich cream soup. Serve a half cup with crisp unsalted crackers to begin a meal, or serve a full cup and a salad as lunch.

Cut the flowerets, from the top of one head of broccoli or cauliflower and save for use as a vegetable. (You may have to use a bit of the tops to make 2 cups.)

Boil:

 1 **cup water**

Add:

 2 **cups chopped fresh or frozen broccoli or cauliflower stems**

Simmer, covered, for 10 minutes (if frozen, for 5 minutes).

Meanwhile, bring to boil:

 2 **cups chicken stock (page 17)**
 1 **teaspoon salt**
 ¼ **teaspoon freshly ground white pepper**
 2 **tablespoons butter**

Mix together in bowl:

 2 **tablespoons cornstarch**
 2 **tablespoons water**

Thicken stock with cornstarch mixture and stir constantly with slotted spoon or whisk until soup is thick and smooth.

Add, still stirring, the drained broccoli or cauliflower and:

 1 **cup heavy cream**
   dash Tabasco sauce

Add salt, freshly ground white pepper, and butter to taste. Use raw broccoli, chopped fine, as a colorful garnish for cauliflower soup or use raw cauliflower, chopped fine, as a garnish for broccoli soup. Good hot or cold.

Black Bean Soup

Whenever we have honey-baked ham at a family party, son-in-law James gets the ham bone, with the promise of black bean soup to come. He's a good cook, and this recipe proves it. The black beans must be picked over even more carefully than black-eyes. Look for small stones.

In bowl, cover with water (1 inch over beans) and soak overnight:

 2 **pounds dried black beans**

Melt in large dutch oven:

 6 **tablespoons bacon drippings**

Sauté in drippings:

 3½ **cups chopped onion**
 4 **large garlic cloves, minced**

Add:

 2 **medium carrots, scrubbed and chopped fine**
 1 **28-ounce can tomatoes, all mashed fine**
 1 **ham bone, preferably honey-baked, with meat scraps**
  left on

Drain and rinse the beans, add them to the above mixture, cover with water, and simmer all day, adding water if necessary. Stir frequently.

Puree about half the cooked beans in a food processor and then return to Dutch oven. Add enough water to make a thick soup. Add salt and the freshly ground pepper to taste.

Serve with chopped onion, sour cream or sherry, and lots of crisp crackers or toasted bagel rings.

Poultry

Southern Fried Chicken • Charles' Crispy Fried Chicken • Smothered Chicken • Baked Chicken • Lemon Baked Chicken • Baked Chicken Parmesan • Louisiana Chicken Perloo • Louisiana Chicken Thighs • Sautéed Chicken Livers • Herbed Chicken in Creamy Wine Sauce • Company Chicken • Chicken 'n' Dumplin's, Granny Lupo Style • Chicken Pan Pie • Barbecued Chicken • Grilled Chicken Patties with Almond Sauce • Baked Quail • Deep-Fried Quail • Pan-Fried Quail

Chicken, chicken, and more chicken. On the farm, we raised them and we ate them. Even today, for taste and for your health, chicken is still king—or queen.

Recipes today feature more broiled or baked chicken than the old-fashioned pan-fried—all of it is good, but you can't really beat southern fried chicken. Pull the skin off and substitute vegetable oil for lard if you must—it will be *almost* as good.

Southern Fried Chicken

MAKES 3 TO 4 SERVINGS

This is probably your southern grandmother's way of frying chicken, and was Mary Mac's best-selling entree for thirty years. Today our customers prefer crispy fried chicken (see next recipe). Either way is delicious!

Cut up:

> 1   **3-pound fryer**

You will have 2 breasts, 2 thighs, 2 drumsticks, and 2 wings. Reserve the backbone and any fat to make chicken stock (page 17). You will also have the giblets.

Rinse off the chicken pieces and giblets and pat dry. Sprinkle lightly with salt and freshly ground pepper. Set aside for 15 minutes or seal in plastic bag overnight in the refrigerator.

Place in bowl:

> ¾   **cup buttermilk**

In another bowl, prepare seasoned flour:

> 2   **cups all-purpose flour**
> 1   **teaspoon salt**
> ½   **teaspoon freshly ground white pepper**

Heat to 375° in heavy 12-inch frying pan:

> 1   **cup lard**

The temperature of the lard is very important; it should be hot enough to make a drop of water sizzle when dropped in.

Dip the chicken pieces and giblets quickly into the buttermilk, then into the flour. Be sure each piece is well covered with flour. Lay out all the floured chicken pieces and floured giblets on a tray in preparation for frying.

A 12-inch frying pan should hold one fryer (8 pieces). Place the large pieces of chicken in the frying pan first and then fit the smaller pieces around them, putting aside the giblets.

Cover frying pan, reduce heat to medium, and brown all pieces well on one side, 8 to 10 minutes. Turn pieces over, add giblets, cover, and brown all pieces well again, 8 to 10 minutes.

The final step is the secret to this wonderful southern fried chicken. Add slowly and carefully to the chicken:

    ½   **cup water**

Return cover and steam for 5 minutes. Remove cover and turn pieces over once again to make the crust crisp. Remove chicken to warm platter.

Make:

    4   **cups fried chicken gravy, (page 206)**

Serve fried chicken with steamed rice and gravy.

Charles' Crispy Fried Chicken

Charles Poole, our nighttime chef, produced this recipe two years ago as an alternative to our original fried chicken. (See previous recipe.) It has proved to be even more popular than the buttermilk-soaked variety and is both easier and quicker to prepare. Charles and I have taught this recipe in various local shows and the participants loved it.

Cut:

> 3–3½ lb. fryer into 8 pieces and rinse under running water; pat dry

Sprinkle:

> Salt and white pepper over chicken and set aside 10 minutes

Fill:

> 12-inch frying pan or deep fryer half full with vegetable oil. Heat to 325°.

Combine:

> 1   cup tepid water
> 1   teaspoon salt
> ½   teaspoon white pepper
> 1   cup all-purpose flour
> 2   drops yellow food coloring

Place chicken pieces in this batter

Combine:

> 1   cup all-purpose flour
> 1   teaspoon salt
> ½   teaspoon white pepper

Lift chicken from first batter, roll in second mixture; shake off excess flour. Fry about 8 minutes on each side. Drain well on paper towels.

Smothered Chicken

MAKES 3 TO 4 SERVINGS

This works well with leftover fried chicken—if you ever have any!

Prepare:

> **southern fried chicken (page 38)**
> 4 **cups fried chicken gravy (page 206)**

When making fried chicken gravy, add to roux 4 cups of milk in place of water, stock, or cream.

Preheat oven to 325°.

Place chicken in 2-quart baking pan; pour gravy over chicken and bake, covered, for 15 to 20 minutes. Milk will soak into chicken crust. The gravy is also delicious on hot biscuits.

Baked Chicken

Rinse well:

1   6- to 7-pound hen

Remove and set aside neck and giblets and clean out cavity.

Place neck and giblets in separate saucepan and add:

2   cups salted water

Simmer, covered, for 1 hour. The giblets and giblet stock will be used later to make chicken gravy. Preheat oven to 325°.

Sprinkle hen, inside and out, with salt and freshly ground pepper. Place hen in heavy Dutch oven and add:

2   cups water

Cover and bake for 1½ hours. Add water if necessary. Test with fork for tenderness and remove to a baking pan. Save chicken stock for gravy. Raise oven temperature to 400°.

Brush hen with:

1   tablespoon melted butter

Return hen to oven and bake for 10 minutes before serving.

Remove neck and giblets from pot and chop the meat to add to chicken gravy.

Make:

2   cups baked chicken gravy (page 204)

Served baked chicken with chicken dressing (page 236), chicken gravy, and cranberry sauce.

Lemon Baked Chicken

Rinse well and pat dry:

chicken pieces (select the pieces your family prefers)

Sprinkle with:

lemon-seasoned salt
freshly ground pepper

Set aside 15 minutes or place in plastic bag overnight in refrigerator.

Preheat oven to 325 to 350°.

Place chicken pieces in shallow ovenproof dish, not touching each other. Sprinkle over the chicken:

garlic, rosemary, thyme, or marjoram (any herb your family likes)

Top with:

bits of butter
paprika
thinly sliced lemon

Cover with lid or aluminum foil. Bake 30 to 40 minutes or until chicken is easily pierced with fork. Remove lid.

Add:

1   **tablespoon dry white wine per piece (optional)**

Bake, uncovered, for 10 minutes.

Baked Chicken Parmesan

Delicious and different with Parmesan sauce.

Rinse well and cut in half:

> 1   2½- to 3-pound fryer

Remove backbone so each half will lie flat. Save backbones to make chicken stock (page 17).

Sprinkle with:

> 1   teaspoon salt
> ½   teaspoon freshly ground black pepper
> 2   tablespoons apple cider vinegar

Let sit about 15 minutes at room temperature or, covered, overnight in the refrigerator. Then pour off vinegar. Preheat oven to 325°.

Brush chicken on both sides with:

> 2   tablespoons melted butter

Sprinkle on both sides with:

> **juice of 1 lemon**

Place in ungreased baking pan, skin side down, and bake 15 minutes. Turn chicken, brush with pan drippings, and bake for another 15 minutes or until tender. Raise oven temperature to 350°.

If skin side has not browned, sprinkle lightly with:

> **paprika**

Return to oven and bake for 3 minutes. Serve with Parmesan sauce (page 212).

Louisiana Chicken Perloo

Perloo is a Deep-South term, probably African in origin, meaning a stew with rice cooked in it. This recipe originally came from a Baptist church dinner in Butler, Georgia. This is a recipe for hungry people.

Place in large Dutch oven:

2	cups chicken stock (page 17)
3	cups diagonally sliced celery
2	cups thinly sliced white onion
2	cups thinly sliced green bell pepper
½	teaspoon chopped jalapeño
1	large garlic clove, minced
1	16-ounce can tomatoes, drained and chopped, juice reserved

Cook mixture slowly for 10 minutes.

Add:

2	cups sliced raw chicken meat
1	small bay leaf, crushed
½	teaspoon dried marjoram
½	teaspoon dried thyme
½	teaspoon salt
2	cups water
1	cup raw rice
1	tablespoon dried parsley
2	knockwursts, sliced thin

Cook, covered, over medium heat for 20 to 30 minutes, stirring occasionally.

If mixture begins to thicken, add:

tomato juice

Serve topped with chopped pecans.

Louisiana Chicken Thighs

Some trouble, but delicious.

Rinse:

> 8   **medium-sized chicken thighs**

Melt in heavy skillet or Dutch oven:

> 1   **stick butter**

Prepare seasoned flour on sheet of wax paper:

> ½   **cup all-purpose flour**
> **salt and freshly ground black pepper**

Flour each thigh, patting well to get flour all over each piece. Shake off excess, then place in pan of melted butter over *low* heat. Brown lightly on each side. Remove thighs to baking pan. Preheat oven to 350°.

In pan used to brown chicken or in a separate pan, brown:

> ½   **pound sweet Italian sausage**

Cut into 2-inch pieces and add sausage to chicken.

In the same pan or, if the butter has browned too much, in a pan with ½ stick fresh butter, brown:

> 6   **spring onions, chopped**
> ¼   **banana pepper (careful!), chopped**
> ½   **yellow bell pepper, chopped**
> 2   **garlic cloves, chopped**

Pour the pepper mixture over the chicken and sausage.

Add to the frying pan:

1   14½-ounce can tomatoes, chopped fine

Simmer for 2 minutes, then pour into the baking dish. If you do not have at least ½ inch of juice in the baker, rinse your frying pan out with a little water and pour it into the baking pan. Sprinkle lightly with salt and freshly ground pepper.

Cover and bake for 30 minutes. Remove from oven and taste the sauce. Add salt if necessary. Bake for about 10 minutes more, uncovered, or reheat just before serving.

Sautéed Chicken Livers

MAKES 4 TO 6 SERVINGS

Clean and wash:

2   pounds chicken livers

Sprinkle with salt and freshly ground white pepper and let sit 30 minutes. Preheat oven to 350°.

Mix in small baking pan:

2   cups all-purpose flour
1   teaspoon salt
¼   teaspoon freshly ground white pepper

Dredge each liver through the seasoned flour, being careful to coat it. Shake off excess flour.

Grease heavy aluminum baking pan with lard. Place livers in pan and sprinkle with paprika. Bake for 30 minutes or until brown.

These are delicious served with steamed rice, Creole rice, or wild rice and chicken gravy.

Herbed Chicken in Creamy Wine Sauce (The Wolds' Favorite Chicken Dish)

MAKES 4 SERVINGS

Daughter Judy's standard is perfection, in cooking or career, and she comes close to it in this recipe. Judy says the herbs may be measured generously— follow your family's preference.

Melt in heavy pan with tight lid:

   4   tablespoons butter

Add:

   4   5-ounce boned chicken breast halves

Sauté for about 10 minutes on each side.

In a bowl, mix:

   **4   cups chicken bouillon dissolved in 1½ cups hot water
         or use 1½ cups chicken stock (page 17)**
   ½   teaspoon salt
   ½   teaspoon freshly ground white pepper
   3   tablespoons chopped chives
   1½   tablespoons chopped fresh parsley
   ½   teaspoon dried thyme
   ¼   teaspoon dried rosemary

Add the herb mixture to the sautéed chicken breasts, cover, and simmer for 15 to 20 minutes. Remove breasts and set aside.

Sift into the liquid:

   3   tablespoons all-purpose flour

Stir constantly with wire whisk until the mixture thickens.

Add:

1   cup sour cream or heavy cream
½   cup Sauternes or other white wine

Serve on rice. Pour gravy over chicken breasts and sprinkle each serving with toasted almonds.

Company Chicken

MAKES 2 SERVINGS

Cut in half:

1   2- to 3-pound fryer

Remove the backbone so the halves will lie flat. Save backbones to make chicken stock (page 17). Rinse off and clean. Place in flat dish or pan.

Mix well:

1   cup soy sauce
1   cup dry sherry
½   cup French dressing with garlic (page 193)
1   teaspoon salt
½   teaspoon freshly ground white pepper
½   teaspoon garlic powder

Pour mixture over chicken and marinate for 1 hour or more. Lift out chicken and drain. Place in greased baking pan and seal with aluminum foil. Preheat oven to 325°.

Bake for about 1 hour, until fork-tender. Remove foil. Drain off and discard juice.

Dribble some melted butter over chicken and brown under broiler or in oven preheated to 450° for a few minutes just before serving. Serve with pecan dressing (page 236).

Chicken 'n' Dumplin's, Granny Lupo Style

Granny Lupo lived with us for many years before she died. She loved to cook, and this is one of the dishes she did best. All six children and my husband loved dumplin's made this way.

Chicken 'n' dumplin's has always been a regular stick-to-the-ribs meal for us, especially in winter. The old-fashioned way to make dumpling dough was to make a well in the middle of the flour in your wooden mixing bowl and work into the egg mixture whatever flour it would take up. However, different days, different ways.

Beat well:

    1   egg

Add:

    1   tablespoon water
    ½   teaspoon salt
    1   teaspoon melted butter
    1   drop yellow food coloring

Add slowly to the egg mixture:

    1   cup all-purpose flour

Stir the mixture around and around your mixing bowl until it makes a ball. Cover the ball and let sit in the refrigerator 30 minutes. This is called "resting" the dough.

Turn dough out onto a lightly floured board or marble slab and knead. It may take up to another ¼ cup of flour to make it easy to handle. Roll out dough paper-thin and cut into strips 1 inch wide by 4 inches long.

Place in large pot:

4 cups chicken stock (page 17)
  salt to taste
¼ teaspoon freshly ground white pepper
1 drop yellow food coloring

Bring chicken stock to a rolling boil and slowly lower each strip of dough into stock, keeping stock at high boil. This will keep the strips from sticking together. Then simmer, covered, for about 30 minutes and taste for tenderness.

Stock should be somewhat thick from excess flour on the dumplings. However, if thickening is needed, mix together:

2 tablespoons cornstarch
2 tablespoons water

Add cornstarch mixture to stock while stirring.

Heat and stir in just before serving:

½ cup light cream

Serve with boiled chicken pieces or with leftover baked chicken pulled off the bone and dropped into stock with dumplings just before serving.

Chicken Pan Pie

This is the southern chicken pan pie. It does not *have vegetables in it!*

Place in 2-quart pot:

1	**3-pound fryer** *or* **1 5-pound hen, cleaned and quartered**
4	**cups water**
1	**teaspoon salt**
2	**ribs celery**

Cover and simmer until meat is tender, about 45 to 60 minutes for the chicken, 60 to 75 minutes for the hen. Remove chicken from stock and pull meat from bones. Save chicken stock for gravy. Remove sinews, skin, and any pieces of fat. Cut meat into 1-inch cubes.

Make:

4	**cups baked chicken gravy (page 204)**

Place chicken cubes in 2-quart baking dish and cover with gravy. Preheat oven to 400°.

Make:

½	**pastry recipe (page 280)**

Roll out pastry to size of baking dish, top dish with pastry, and crimp edges. Cut several vent holes in pastry, making a fancy pattern.

Bake until crust is done, about 30 minutes.

Barbecued Chicken

MAKES 2 SERVINGS

This is good oven-barbecued or cooked outside on the grill. If you are grilling outdoors, be sure the charcoal is burned down until gray before cooking.

Rinse well and cut in half:

1   2½- to 3-pound fryer

Remove backbone so each half will lie flat. Save backbones to make chicken stock (page 17).

Sprinkle chicken with:

1   teaspoon salt
½   teaspoon freshly ground black pepper
2   tablespoons apple cider vinegar

Let sit for about 15 minutes at room temperature or, covered, overnight in the refrigerator. Preheat oven to 350° if barbecuing in the oven.

Prepare:

1   cup barbecue sauce (page 200)

Place the vinegared chicken over low fire or place in a baking pan in oven. Cook for 10 minutes on each side, then brush one side with barbecue sauce, turn over toward heat, and cook for 10 minutes more. Then brush other side with barbecue sauce, turn over toward heat, and cook for 10 minutes again.

Chicken should now be very tender and smelling wonderful. Turn and brush again with sauce and finish off quickly for 10 minutes over hot charcoal or at 400° in the oven. Do not burn, but a few charred pieces add to the flavor. Serve with remaining barbecue sauce which has been warmed.

Grilled Chicken Patties with Almond Sauce

MAKES 4 SERVINGS

Melt in small pan:

    1   **tablespoon margarine**

Sauté in margarine:

    1   **cup finely chopped onion**

Place in large bowl:

    2   **cups chopped cooked white and dark chicken meat**
    2   **tablespoons chicken stock (page 17)**

Beat together in separate bowl:

    1   **egg**
    1   **tablespoon water**

Add beaten egg to chicken. Stir in sautéed onion.

Season with:

    ½   **teaspoon celery salt**
    1   **teaspoon salt**
    ½   **teaspoon freshly ground white pepper**
        dash Tabasco sauce

Pinch off walnut-size pieces of patty mixture and pat out flat. Cook on lightly greased hot grill or in lightly greased heavy frying pan. Brown quickly, turn over, and brown other side. Remove from pan or grill.

To make almond sauce, place in small baking pan:

¼ **cup almond slices**
2 **tablespoons melted butter**

Toast almonds quickly under broiler until brown. Remove and add:

2 **tablespoons chicken stock (page 17)**

If your family likes it, a bit of dry white wine is good in this sauce. Serve sauce with patties.

Baked Quail

MAKES 5 SERVINGS

Preheat oven to 350°.

Rinse, pat dry, and sprinkle with salt and freshly ground pepper:

10 **7- to 9-ounce whole quail (thawed if necessary)**

Place in buttered baking pan and add:

10 **tablespoons water**

Seal pan with tight lid of aluminum foil. Bake for 30 to 45 minutes, until tender.

Glaze with pan drippings or melted muscadine jelly (page xvi) for just a few minutes in 450° oven.

Mix toasted, salted pecans with cooked rice, melted butter, and chopped fresh parsley for an excellent side dish to serve with this.

Deep-Fried Quail

Because they spoil easily, the quail found in most grocery stores are usually frozen. Sometimes they are sold fresh, or you may be lucky enough to have a hunting friend bring you some (dressed, let us hope).

If necessary, thaw in room-temperature water:

10   7- to 9-ounce whole quail

Rinse under tap water. If quail have not been split, cut partially down the backbone so the birds will lie flat.

Sprinkle each bird with salt and freshly ground pepper.

Heat to 350° in Dutch oven:

4   cups vegetable oil

Add additional oil if needed to make cooking oil 4 inches deep in pot.

Prepare seasoned flour in bowl:

3   cups all-purpose flour
3   teaspoons salt
1   teaspoon freshly ground white pepper

Quail is such a delicate meat it does not require a heavy coating. Dredge the whole bird through the seasoned flour, shake off excess flour, and drop bird into oil. Do not overcrowd. Quail cook quickly, in about 10 to 12 minutes.

Cream gravy (page 208) made with milk or cream is especially delicious with deep-fried quail.

Serve over wild rice or steamed rice mixed with a few chopped pecans and pimiento bits. Muscadine jelly (page xvi) also goes well with quail.

Pan-Fried Quail

For family, it is easier to pan-fry quail and make quail gravy from the drippings than to deep-fry it.

Heat to 350° in heavy 12-inch frying pan:

2   cups vegetable oil

Prepare seasoned flour in bowl:

3   cups all-purpose flour
3   teaspoons salt
1   teaspoon freshly ground white pepper

Dredge through seasoned flour:

10 7 to 9-ounce whole quail (thawed if necessary)

Fry in oil for 5 to 6 minutes, turning to brown all over. Then remove quail to a baking dish. Preheat oven to 350°.

To make quail gravy, pour oil out of frying pan into heatproof measuring cup and return 4 tablespoons to pan. Loosen browned dripping bits in bottom of pan.

Add, stirring over very low heat until brown:

4   tablespoons all-purpose flour

Add slowly, stirring constantly:

1   cup light cream
1   teaspoon salt
½   teaspoon freshly ground white pepper

Taste and reseason if necessary. If too thick, add water. Pour the quail gravy over the quail in the baking dish and bake for about 10 minutes.

Meats

Fancy Hamburger Pie • Hamburger Pie with Corn Pone Topping • Creole Beef and Macaroni • Spaghetti with Italian Meat Sauce • Mexican Chili with Beans • Salisbury Steak • Meat Loaf • Steak Strips for Two • Beef Pot Roast • Roast Beef • Bell Peppered Beef • Beef Tips with Mandarin Sauce • Beef and Bean Sprouts • Beef Pot Pie • Braised Beef Tips • Beef Stew • Country Fried Steak in Gravy • Beef Turnover • Sautéed Liver • Smothered Liver and Onions • Baked Pork Chops Babs • Baked Pork Chops • Honey Spareribs • Pork Kabobs • Deep-Fried Pork Bits • Pork Roast • Barbecued Pork • Streak O'Lean • Sunday Baked Ham • Country Ham with Redeye Gravy • Brunswick Stew • Veal Chops Parmesan

I suppose this is a good place to brag about our beautiful supermarkets. The meat displays are gorgeous, and there are many items ready to cook. However, people who are interested in cooking (people who buy cookbooks) still like to do their own thing. I have learned to live with some of the prepared meats, but there is no way, so far, that the meat markets or the frozen counters can do as well as you can in your own kitchen.

Beef

Fancy Hamburger Pie

Bring to boil:

    1   **quart water**

Add:

    ½   **cup wild rice**

Simmer for 20 minutes and add:

    ½   **cup long-grain white rice**
    1   **teaspoon salt**

Simmer until grains are softened, about 10 minutes. Drain.

Melt in heavy skillet:

    1   **tablespoon butter**

Add:

    1   **medium onion, chopped**

Brown, then add:

    1   **pound lean ground beef**

Stir with potato masher to break up lumps until beef is in smooth grains. Preheat oven to 300°.

Add the rice mixture and:

       1   tablespoon chicken base*
       1   teaspoon salt
       ½   teaspoon freshly ground black pepper
       1   bay leaf (optional)
       3   ounces chopped fresh or canned mushrooms

Pour into buttered ovenproof dish and top with:

unbaked pastry (page 280) or flaky canned biscuit pulled apart in layers

Be sure pastry top is ½ to 1 inch larger than dish and prick it in several places to allow steam to escape. Bake 45 minutes.

---

*Chicken base is a commercial preparation of reduced chicken broth, available in gourmet spice sections. Check label carefully—if salt is listed first, that is the prime ingredient, and you are most interested in chicken. A dry base is very advantageous in dishes such as this, where you do not want to add more liquid.

Hamburger Pie
with Corn Pone Topping

The corn pone topping makes a world of difference to this dish.

Brown in heavy 10-inch frying pan:

> 2 pounds ground beef
> 1 teaspoon salt
> ½ teaspoon freshly ground black pepper

Remove with slotted spoon into ovenproof casserole.

Add:

> 1 5½-ounce can whole-grain yellow corn, drained
> ½ cup tomato sauce
> dash Tabasco sauce
> dash Worcestershire sauce
> salt and freshly ground pepper to taste

Make in separate bowl:

> 1 cup cornbread muffin batter (page 227)

Thin cornbread mixture with:

> 3 tablespoons buttermilk, milk, or water

Preheat oven to 350°. Pour cornbread mixture very carefully over the beef mixture. Spread evenly. Bake until corn pone topping is done, 25 to 30 minutes.

Creole Beef and Macaroni

Cook according to package directions:

    1   **8-ounce package macaroni, any shape**

Drain and rinse well with cold water.

Brown in heavy 10-inch frying pan:

    2   **pounds ground chuck**
    1   **teaspoon salt**
    ½   **teaspoon freshly ground black pepper**

Skim off fat. Preheat oven to 400°.

Make:

    4   **cups creole sauce (page 208)**

In 2-quart buttered baking dish, alternate layers of half the macaroni, half the meat mixture, and half the creole sauce. Repeat layers.

Top mixture with:

    ½   **cup grated Parmesan or Cheddar cheese**

Bake until sauce is bubbling and cheese has melted, 15 to 20 minutes.

Spaghetti with Italian Meat Sauce

Over the years southerners have adopted this dish as one of their own.

Brown in 10-inch frying pan:

2	pounds lean ground chuck
2	teaspoons salt

Skim off fat and place cooked meat in heavy Dutch oven.

Add:

1	cup chopped white onion
1	cup chopped celery
½	cup chopped green bell pepper
6	garlic cloves, chopped
2	16-ounce cans tomatoes, chopped, with juice
1	small bay leaf
¼	teaspoon dried thyme
¼	teaspoon dried basil
½	teaspoon dried oregano
½	teaspoon dried marjoram
	dash Tabasco sauce

Simmer slowly, covered, for 30 minutes. Taste and reseason if necessary.

Add to hot spaghetti sauce:

1	cup sliced fresh mushrooms (optional)
½	cup red wine (optional)

Simmer for 10 minutes more.

Cook as directed on package:

1	pound spaghetti

Serve meat sauce over spaghetti, topped with grated Parmesan cheese. Don't forget the garlic toast.

Mexican Chili with Beans

MAKES 4 TO 6 SERVINGS

I have a newspaper columnist friend who is always ready to fight the addition of beans to this dish. With or without beans, chili is a popular cold-night supper. Goes well on hot dogs too.

Sauté in heavy 12-inch frying pan:

2	pounds ground chuck, broken up
1	teaspoon salt

Skim off fat and add:

1	cup chopped white onion
1	24-ounce can tomatoes, chopped, with juice, hard cores removed
2	garlic cloves, sliced thin
3	tablespoons chili powder
½	teaspoon hot red pepper flakes
1	teaspoon paprika
2	teaspoons salt
1	teaspoon freshly ground black pepper

Simmer mixture for about 30 minutes.

Add and mix in:

1	16-ounce can red chili beans, drained

Simmer slowly for another 30 minutes. If mixture gets too thick, thin with ¼ cup of water at a time. Taste. Reseason with chili powder and/or salt and freshly ground pepper to taste.

Salisbury Steak

Place in bowl:

    1½ cups water
    6   bran muffins (page 221)

Soak for 2 minutes. Squeeze out excess water and place in 2-quart mixing bowl.

Add to muffins and mix well:

    1   tablespoon grated onion
    1   beaten egg
    2   pounds ground chuck
    2   teaspoons salt
    1   teaspoon freshly ground black pepper

Preheat oven to 350°. Divide meat mixture into six portions. With wet hands, form into six thick oval patties, dipping your hands into water each time. Bake on greased baking sheet for about 30 minutes.

Save drippings for beef gravy (page 202) with onions or mushrooms.

Meat Loaf

Prepare:

Salisbury steak mixture (page 66)

Preheat oven to 350°. Place mixture in greased and floured loaf pan. Work mixture into pan with wet hands. To eliminate air holes, drop the pan forcefully on wooden countertop several times. Smooth the top into a rounded loaf shape.

Bake for 45 to 60 minutes. Do not let meat loaf get overdone; it will dry out. Allow to cool for 10 to 15 minutes after you remove it from oven. The texture will set, and you may slice it more evenly.

Serve with beef gravy (page 202) or tomato sauce (page 216).

Steak Strips for Two

MAKES 2 SERVINGS

Melt in heavy 12-inch frying pan:

½   stick butter

Add:

1   pound sirloin steak, sliced ¼ inch thick across the grain

Brown slightly and turn over.

Add:

2   fresh tomatoes, peeled and cut into wedges
1   bunch scallions, cleaned and cut into 1-inch lengths
1   tablespoon soy sauce
3   tablespoons white wine
    salt and freshly ground black pepper to taste

Cook for about 2 minutes, turn mixture over, and cook for another 2 minutes. Serve over Chinese noodles or rice. Garlic toast also goes well with this.

Try serving your green salad in two large flat soup bowls topped with steaming steak strips. A wonderful one-dish meal.

Beef Pot Roast

Beef chuck makes a good sturdy pot roast.

Preheat oven to 300°.

Rub with salt and pepper:

> 1   **3- to 4-pound chuck roast, about 2 inches thick, with a small bone**

Place chuck in Dutch oven and add:

> ⅔   **cup water**

Cover and bake for 2 hours.

Add to Dutch oven:

> **4 to 6 very small carrots *or* 3 larger carrots cut into 1-inch pieces, peeled**
> **4 to 6 small onions, peeled**
> **4 to 6 new potatoes, 1 to 1½ inches in diameter, peeled**

Cover and bake for 30 minutes. Remove from oven and check. Meat should be fork-tender, vegetables well done. Place meat and vegetables in 2-quart baking dish. Raise oven temperature to 350°.

Place Dutch oven with juice over medium heat on top of stove and make beef gravy by thickening with 1 tablespoon flour for each cup of juice. Stir continuously until thick and lump-free.

Pour gravy over pot roast, return to oven, cover, and bake for 10 minutes.

Roast Beef

This is the best method for roasting most cuts of beef. Only prime cuts or well-larded meat should be dry-roasted.

Preheat oven to 400°.

Rinse:

    1   **4-pound sirloin tip roast**

Pat dry and rub with:

    1   **teaspoon salt**
    1   **teaspoon coarsely ground black pepper**

Place meat in heavy Dutch oven and add:

    ⅔   **cup water**

Cover and bake for 15 minutes. Reduce oven temperature to 350° and bake, covered, for 1 hour. Test with fork for tenderness. If a two-pronged kitchen fork goes in easily, the roast is medium well done.

Remove roast to warm plate. There should be enough stock to serve with roast or to make clear beef gravy (page 201). If not, add to Dutch oven:

    ½   **cup water**
    ½   **teaspoon Kitchen Bouquet**

Scrape sides of pot down into stock and simmer a few minutes. Add salt to taste.

Serve gravy over slices of beef roast or on the side.

Bell Peppered Beef

Slice into very thin strips:

2   pounds lean beef (round steak or top sirloin preferred), with fat removed
1   large clove garlic

Melt in 10-inch frying pan:

2   tablespoons margarine

Add beef and garlic to pan and season with:

1   teaspoon salt
½   teaspoon freshly ground black pepper

Sauté gently for 10 minutes.

Add to beef strips:

2   medium-sized green bell peppers, sliced into thin strips
1   cup sliced fresh mushrooms (optional)

Simmer, covered, for another 5 minutes. Add salt and Tabasco sauce to taste.

To thicken gravy, mix together in separate bowl:

3   tablespoons cornstarch
1   cup water

Add cornstarch mixture to the frying pan along with:

½   teaspoon Kitchen Bouquet

Stir well and simmer for 3 minutes more.

Serve immediately over steamed rice or fried noodles.

Beef Tips with Mandarin Sauce

Prepare:

> **braised beef tips (page 74), without the beef gravy**

After browning beef cubes, add:

> 1   **recipe mandarin sauce (page 213)**

Set aside bean sprouts and mushrooms for later use. Cover and simmer for 1 hour or until tips are tender.

Rinse and add:

> 2   **cups bean sprouts, bamboo shoots, or water chestnuts**
> 1   **cup sliced fresh mushrooms**
> ¼   **pound snow peas, trimmed**

Simmer for 5 minutes.

Serve over steamed rice or fried noodles.

Beef and Bean Sprouts

Melt in 10-inch frying pan:

½ cup margarine

Sauté in margarine:

2 pounds lean beef chuck, cut into julienne strips about
⅛ inch by 3 inches

Pour into 2-quart saucepan:

1 cup very strong tea
2 cups beef stock (page 16) or canned beef broth
2 tablespoons soy sauce
¼ cup Burgundy or other red wine
½ teaspoon salt
¼ teaspoon freshly ground white pepper
¼ tablespoon sugar
⅛ teaspoon hot red pepper flakes

Bring liquid to a boil. Add:

½ cup thinly sliced celery
½ cup thinly sliced white onion
1 garlic clove, sliced thin
½ cup thinly sliced fresh mushrooms

Simmer for 5 minutes. Add beef strips.

Mix together in separate bowl:

3 tablespoons cornstarch
3 tablespoons water

Thicken beef mixture with cornstarch mixture.

Pick over and rinse:

½ **pound fresh bean sprouts**
½ **pound snowpeas or chopped broccoli tips**

Pour over the bean sprouts and snowpeas or broccoli:

4 **cups boiling water**

Drain water off immediately and add vegetables to beef mixture. Simmer for 5 minutes. Taste and reseason if necessary. Serve over steamed rice or fried noodles.

Beef Pot Pie

MAKES 4 TO 6 SERVINGS

Prepare:

beef stew (page 76)

Pour into 2-quart baking dish. Be sure gravy almost covers the meat and vegetables. If necessary, add water.

Preheat oven to 425°.

Prepare:

½ **recipe pastry (page 280)**

Roll pastry out very thin on lightly floured board or marble slab. Cut to size of baking dish. Top dish with pastry and seal edges. Cut several vent holes in pastry, making a fancy pattern.

Bake until top is golden brown, about 20 minutes.

Braised Beef Tips

Cut into 1-inch cubes:

> 2   pounds top sirloin

Sprinkle with:

> 1   teaspoon salt
> ½   teaspoon freshly ground black pepper

Melt in 12-inch frying pan:

> ½   cup margarine

Brown the beef cubes in the margarine over low heat, about 20 minutes, stirring often.

Add:

> 1   cup chopped scallion or white onion
> 2   cups water
> 1   teaspoon salt

Cover and simmer gently for 1 hour. Test with fork for tenderness; when meat is done, remove to warm bowl with slotted spoon while preparing gravy from beef stock.

To make beef gravy, skim fat from top of the beef stock. Add salt to taste.

Add to beef stock:

> enough water to make 2 cups liquid
> ½   teaspoon Kitchen Bouquet
> dash Tabasco sauce

To thicken, mix together in separate bowl:

3   tablespoons cornstarch
3   tablespoons water

Add cornstarch mixture to stock and stir constantly for a smooth gravy. If lumpy, strain and return to pan.

Return meat to gravy and simmer gently for 10 minutes. Add salt, freshly ground pepper, and Tabasco sauce to taste. Meat should be quite tender.

Add:

2   tablespoons red wine (optional)

To serve over noodles or rice, prepare according to package instructions:

1   8-ounce package noodles or macaroni, any shape, *or* ½ cup rice

Garnish with chopped fresh parsley.

Beef tips are delicious with spinach noodles, sautéed mushrooms, and the beef gravy with wine.

Beef Stew

This is another variation of braised beef tips.

Cut into 1-inch cubes:

> **2   pounds top sirloin**

Sprinkle with:

> **1   teaspoon salt**
> **½   teaspoon freshly ground black pepper**

Melt in 12-inch frying pan:

> **½   cup margarine**

Brown the beef cubes in the margarine over low heat, stirring often, for about 20 minutes.

Add to beef cubes:

> **2   cups water**
> **1   teaspoon salt**
> **4 to 6 small tender carrots, peeled and cut into bite-size pieces**
> **4 to 6 small onions, peeled and cut into bite-size pieces**
> **2 to 3 Idaho potatoes, peeled and cut into bite-size pieces**

Cover and simmer gently for 1 hour. Test meat with fork for tenderness; when meat is done, remove meat and vegetables to warm bowl with slotted spoon while preparing gravy.

To make beef gravy, skim fat from top of the beef stock. Add water to make 2 cups liquid. Add to beef stock:

½   teaspoon Kitchen Bouquet
dash Tabasco sauce
salt to taste

To thicken, mix together in separate bowl:

3   tablespoons cornstarch
3   tablespoons water

Add cornstarch mixture to stock and then return meat and vegetables to gravy.

For more color when serving, sprinkle stew with:

1   teaspoon dried parsley *or* 2 tablespoons chopped fresh parsley (optional)

Or add to the gravy:

½   cup cooked tiny fresh or canned green peas (optional)

Country Fried Steak in Gravy

A favorite of city folks, too. Allow one 4-ounce steak per person. Big eaters will probably want two.

Mix together in bowl:

> 1 **cup all-purpose flour**
> 1 **teaspoon salt**
> ¼ **teaspoon freshly ground black pepper**

Dredge in seasoned flour:

> **4 to 6 4-ounce cubed steaks***

Shake off excess flour.

Melt in heavy 12-inch frying pan:

> ½ **cup vegetable oil or butter**

Brown the steaks for 3 minutes on each side over medium heat and remove to baking dish. Preheat oven to 350°.

Brown in the same pan, using the beef drippings:

---

*A good grade of round steak or sirloin is necessary. If your market does not have steaks of this quality already cubed (put through a cubing machine), you may do as I saw my mother do 50 years ago—pound a slice of round steak with a wooden mallet. This tenderizes it and then you may cut it in serving-size pieces.

We buy these steaks already cubed, but some markets use a cheaper cut than round steak or sirloin and cube the steak three or four times (with a machine) to make it tender—you pick it up, and it falls apart like hamburger. Not much flavor, either. Hamburger does not work in this recipe.

Stirring constantly, add:

3   tablespoons flour
3   cups water
    Salt and freshly ground pepper to taste

Cook 5 minutes.

Pour gravy over steaks. Bake steaks for 15 to 20 minutes. Serve in gravy with steamed rice or whipped potatoes.

Beef Turnover

These individual pies are one of Mary Mac's best-selling items. Men particularly like them—with lots of gravy, of course.

Brown in heavy 10-inch frying pan:

2	pounds ground chuck
½	cup chopped onion
½	cup chopped green bell pepper
1	teaspoon salt
	dash garlic powder *or* 1 small garlic clove, minced
½	teaspoon freshly ground black pepper

Skim off fat. Cool.

Add:

salt and pepper to taste
dash Worcestershire sauce (optional)
dash Tabasco sauce (optional)

Make:

1	recipe pastry (page 280)

Preheat oven to 400°. Roll pastry out very thin on lightly floured board or marble slab. Cut into eight 6-inch circles. (Use an inverted 6-inch bowl and cut around it for the pattern.)

Divide the cooled meat mixture into eight parts and place on one half of each circle. Fold the pastry over the meat and crimp the edges together with a fork. Prick several vent holes in the upper side with the prongs of a fork.

Place turnovers on lightly greased baking sheet. Bake for about 20 minutes, until the crust is golden brown.

Glaze the turnovers with cream or melted butter.

Serve with beef gravy with mushrooms (page 202).

Sautéed Liver

MAKES 6 SERVINGS

Liver sells well at Mary Mac's, often because only one person in a family likes it, so it is not usually cooked at home. (However, how are you going to teach your children to enjoy all kinds of food if you don't serve it to them?)

Rinse in water:

2   **pounds calf or yearling liver, sliced ¼-inch thick**

Sprinkle each slice with:

salt and freshly ground white pepper

Melt in heavy 12-inch frying pan:

1   **cup margarine or butter**

Sauté liver slices for 3 minutes on each side. Do not overcook. Remove liver to warm platter.

Sauté in same margarine:

1   **large sweet white onion, sliced thin**

Brown onion slices on both sides.

To serve, place sautéed onions on top of or around liver slices.

Smothered Liver and Onions

Calf liver is almost too expensive for most of us. Yearling liver, however, is tender with good flavor.

Rinse in water and pat dry:

    2   **pounds liver, sliced ¼-inch thick**

Mix together:

    1   **cup all-purpose flour**
    1   **teaspoon salt**
    ¼   **teaspoon freshly ground white pepper**

Dredge liver in seasoned flour. Shake off excess.

Melt in heavy frying pan:

    1   **stick butter**

Brown the liver slices quickly over high heat, about 3 minutes on each side. Do not overcook as liver tends to become tough. Remove to a warm platter.

Add to frying pan:

    1   **large onion, sliced thin**

Brown onion and remove to liver platter.

To make gravy, scrape loose the browned bits of flour.

Add to frying pan:

    2   **tablespoons all-purpose flour**

Brown flour slowly and carefully, stirring, being sure not to burn the flour.

Add to pan:

1   cup water

Stir while cooking, until gravy is desired thickness. You may need a bit more water. Add salt and freshly ground white pepper to taste.

Return the liver and onions to the pan and simmer very slowly for about 5 minutes for well-done liver, or serve the gravy on the side. Wonderful served on steamed rice or biscuits.

Pork

Baked Pork Chops Babs

My daughter-in-law, Babs, fixes pork chops for her family in an easy manner in an ovenproof glass baking dish.

Preheat oven to 350°.

Season with salt and freshly ground pepper:

4   6- to 7-ounce pork chops, 1¼ to 1½ inches thick

Lay in ovenproof glass dish.

Place on top of *each* chop:

1   large onion slice

Spoon on top of and around chops:

6   tablespoons raw rice

Spread thickly over chops:

1   16-ounce can stewed tomatoes

Sprinkle with:

> **dried basil**
> **onion salt**
> **freshly ground pepper**

Cover dish tightly and bake for 1½ hours.

Baked Pork Chops

Preheat oven to 350°.

Select:

4 to 8 4-ounce centercut pork chops

Sprinkle chops with:

salt and freshly ground pepper
pinch dried oregano (optional)

To make egg wash, beat together:

1   large egg
2   tablespoons water
     dash Tabasco sauce
     dash Worcestershire sauce

Mix together in separate bowl:

1   cup all-purpose flour
2   teaspoons salt

Dip pork chops in egg wash, then in seasoned flour. Shake off excess flour. Place on heavily greased baking pan. Bake, uncovered, for 30 minutes. Turn over and test with fork for tenderness. If a sharp fork goes in all the way easily, the chops are done. If red juices flow, they're too rare. Raise oven temperature to 400°.

Finish off in oven for about 10 minutes more. Exact time depends on thickness of the chops.

Pour drippings and brown bits into frying pan and make cream gravy (page 208) or serve with hot spiced applesauce.

Honey Spareribs

Allow 1 pound of small spareribs for each person, depending on appetites.

Preheat oven to 300°

Cut into individual ribs and sprinkle with salt:

1   2- to 3-pound rack spareribs

Place in long ovenproof glass dish in one layer. Bake for 1 hour. Reduce oven temperature to 250°.

Mix together:

5   tablespoons honey
2   tablespoons soy sauce
1   tablespoon fresh lemon juice
½   teaspoon ground ginger

Pour honey mixture over ribs and bake for 30 minutes.

Remove dish from oven, drain juice into frying pan, and add:

5   tablespoons vinegar
½   red bell pepper, cut into thin strips
½   yellow bell pepper, cut into thin strips
1   6-ounce can pineapple chunks, drained
3   whole green onions *or* ½ sliced red onion (optional)

Poach the vegetable mixture in the juice for about 3 minutes, just long enough to heat it but retain crispness, and serve over the ribs.

Pork Kabobs

Wooden skewers can be purchased at Oriental and gourmet markets.

Slice into at least 15 ¼-inch-thick slices or bite-sized cubes:

1   **1½- to 2-pound pork tenderloin**

Marinate overnight in refrigerator or 30 minutes at room temperature:

1   **cup garlic wine vinegar**
½   **cup soy sauce**

Drain:

1   **6-ounce can pineapple chunks**

Wash, cut in half, and seed:

1   **large bell pepper**

Cut each half into 5 wedges. Preheat oven to 325°.

Drain marinade from pork and reserve. Alternately thread five wooden skewers with pineapple cubes, pork, and bell pepper.

Place kabobs on baking pan and brush with marinade. Bake for 30 to 40 minutes.

Serve over steamed rice mixed with raisins (presoaked for 10 minutes in hot water).

Deep-Fried Pork Bits

MAKES 4 TO 5 SERVINGS OR
ABOUT 20 HORS D'OEUVRES

Very special either as a dinner entree or hors d'oeuvres.

Trim fat from:

1   **1½-pound pork tenderloin**

Cut pork into 1-inch cubes.

Mix in bowl:

1   **cup soy sauce**
1   **cup dry sherry**
½   **teaspoon freshly ground white pepper**
1   **garlic clove, chopped**
1   **teaspoon salt (optional)**

Place pork cubes in marinade for 30 minutes or cover and refrigerate overnight. Lift from marinade and drain.

Heat to 350° in deep fryer:

3   **cups vegetable oil**

Mix together in separate bowl:

1   **cup all-purpose flour**
2   **teaspoons salt**
1   **teaspoon freshly ground white pepper**

Dredge pork cubes in seasoned flour, shake off excess, and deep-fry in batches until golden. Drain on paper towels.

Serve with sweet and sour sauce (page 215) over rice for an entree or serve on toothpicks for hors d'oeuvres, with either sweet and sour sauce (page 215) or barbecue sauce (page 200) as a dip.

Pork Roast

Preheat oven to 350°.

Rub on both sides with salt and freshly ground black pepper:

   1   **5- to 6-pound Boston pork roast**

Sprinkle with:

   1   **teaspoon dried oregano**

Place roast in heavy Dutch oven and add:

   1   **cup water**
   3   **garlic cloves, peeled**

Cover and bake for 1 hour. Check; if still not tender, raise oven temperature to 375° and bake until tender. Add water if dry. Remove from oven.

To make gravy, set roast on warm platter. Remove garlic. Pour juice left in Dutch oven into 1-quart heatproof measuring cup. Add enough water to make 2 cups of liquid and return to pot. Scrape sides of pot down into liquid.

Mix together in separate bowl:

   2   **tablespoons cornstarch**
       as little water as possible to dissolve cornstarch

Bring liquid to a boil. Add cornstarch mixture slowly, stirring constantly, until thickened. If lumps form, strain and return to pan.

Add:

  ½   **teaspoon Kitchen Bouquet**
   1   **teaspoon salt**
  ½   **teaspoon freshly ground white or black pepper**

Slice pork roast and serve with gravy.

Barbecued Pork

MAKES 6 SERVINGS WITH RIBS OR CHOPS, APPROXIMATELY 15 SERVINGS WITH FRESH HAM

This barbecue recipe can be used for different cuts of pork—ribs, chops, or ham.

Preheat oven to 350°.

Prepare:

2   cups barbecue sauce (page 200)

Select:

12   ½-inch-thick pork ribs *or* 12 ½-inch-thick pork chops *or* 1 14- to 16-pound fresh ham

Place ribs or chops in baking dish. Brush sauce very lightly on all sides and bake for approximately 30 minutes, turning occasionally and brushing lightly with barbecue sauce each time.

Fresh ham is difficult to find unless you have connections with a farm or an interested butcher. Ham already cured with salt or another process does not need this long slow baking. Start fresh ham in oven at 350° for 30 minutes, then reduce heat to 300° for another 3 hours, lightly brushing on barbecue sauce every half hour.

Ribs and chops may be cooked on an outdoor charcoal grill in the same manner. Baste pork ribs or chops frequently and grill for 20 minutes on each side. Keep water handy to extinguish flames or meat will burn.

The fresh ham may be cooked on a spit or in a covered outdoor charcoal grill—timing depends on heat from coals. It needs to cook at a low temperature for 3½ to 4 hours, which is difficult to do on the usual home-style grill. You will have to be very careful about adding more charcoal a little at a time to keep an even heat this long. Make sure you brush on barbecue sauce every 30 minutes, although this odor will bring neighbors a-visiting.

Serve with extra barbecue sauce. The leftovers are good cut up for Brunswick stew (page 94).

Streak O'Lean

MAKES 5 SERVINGS

Streak o'lean is an old-fashioned Depression dish, sometimes called Tennessee fried chicken. Actually streak o'lean is salt pork with a strip of lean meat running through the fat. It is similar to bacon but is cured differently. These days it is difficult to find a butcher who knows streak o'lean and how to slice it. We get ours specially cut at Foster's Meat Stall at the Atlanta Municipal Market. Ask for streak o'lean with the rind cut off and the meat cut into ⅛-inch slices.

Select:

10 long slices streak o'lean or enough for 5 people

Soak slices for 30 minutes in:

1½ cups buttermilk

Heat in heavy 12-inch frying pan:

½   pound lard

Meanwhile, mix in baking pan:

1   cup all-purpose flour
1   teaspoon salt
½   teaspoon freshly ground white pepper

Pick up one piece of streak. Dredge in flour, being sure it is completely covered. Shake off excess flour and place streak in hot lard. When piece begins to crinkle up, quickly turn it over. Cook other pieces in similar fashion. Drain on paper towels.

Serve for lunch or dinner with grits and cream gravy (page 208) as side dishes or serve with cheese soufflé or other egg dishes.

Sunday Baked Ham

The key word in selecting a ham for this classic recipe is cured. Cured hams are injected with a brine solution and hung in a temperature-controlled curing room to preserve or cure before you buy them. A 3 percent (of the total weight) solution makes a fine ham; many dealers add water up to 10 percent or more, which pumps up the weight and supposedly makes the ham more economical to sell. Watch the label—if it says "water added," look for another brand.

Trim the skin and fat leaving about ¼ inch of fat, to about 4 inches from the small end of:

1   14- to 16-pound cured ham

Preheat the oven to 300°. Place ham in heavy covered Dutch oven. Pour over it:

1   16-ounce bottle Coca-Cola (not diet!)

Add:

½   inch water

Cover tightly and bake for 1 hour. Remove cover. Pour over ham:

1   16-ounce can Coca-Cola

Leave uncovered and bake for another 2 hours. Remove from oven. Turn oven off.

Score ham in crisscross pattern. Place in each score:

decorative fruit such as pineapple rings or red cherries

Return to oven and leave in cooling oven until ready to serve (at least 30 minutes). Remove to platter and carve at table.

With carving knife and fork in hand, hold ham firmly with the fork. With a long sharp knife, cut a triangular wedge from the small end of the ham straight down to the bone. Remove this wedge (use for sandwiches later). The center of the ham is now open to you and may be sliced in beautiful pink pieces for your guests.

Brunswick Stew

There is no way to have sho-nuf Brunswick Stew without having barbecued pork, cooked chicken, and barbecue sauce on hand. This is sometimes served with barbecued meat and sometimes as a main dish.

Grind together or chop very fine and set aside:

2   cups barbecued pork
1   cup boiled, boned, and cubed chicken, white and dark
    meat

Melt in Dutch oven:

2   tablespoons margarine

Sauté in margarine:

1   cup chopped onion

Add to onion:

1   16-ounce can tomatoes, mashed, with juice
1   5-ounce can whole-grain white or yellow corn, drained

Simmer 5 minutes; add pork and chicken. Cover and simmer slowly for 1 hour.

Add to mixture:

¼   teaspoon salt
¼   teaspoon freshly ground black pepper
    dash Tabasco sauce
    dash Worcestershire sauce
2   tablespoons barbecue sauce (page 200)
    garlic salt to taste

If mixture seems too dry, add small amount of water. Taste. Add more of the above seasonings if you wish. Some like to add lima beans; we say, please, no lima beans.

I like to eat this with crusy French bread.

Country Ham with Redeye Gravy

MAKES 2 SERVINGS

Country ham is cured with salt, not sugar, and is a favorite breakfast meat with grits, eggs, and biscuits. It is also served for dinner with an assortment of vegetables and breads. Country ham is chewy, salty, and delicious with redeye gravy, which is made from the ham drippings and coffee.

Your butcher will cut country ham steaks, or you can buy packages of sliced steaks in the grocery store. The ham is already smoked, so you are basically heating it for serving.

Remove from package, rinse, and pat dry:

> 1 **8-ounce country ham steak**

Cut off the brown rind around the ham slice, leaving the fat.

Heat heavy frying pan to medium heat and brown ham steaks for 3 to 4 minutes on each side. Remove ham to warm platter. You should have about 1 tablespoon of drippings left in the pan.

Reduce heat to low and add very slowly:

> ½ **cup black coffee**
> ½ **cup water**

Stir well, scraping drippings into gravy. The gravy will be dark red, juicy, and salty.

Serve with ham and grits and soak up gravy with biscuits.

Veal

Veal Chops Parmesan

Preheat oven to 350°.

Melt in heavy frying pan:

3   tablespoons butter

Brown in butter:

4   veal steaks or chops

Remove to baking dish with lid and sprinkle with salt and pepper.

Pour into the frying pan:

½   cup dry white wine

Mix well with drippings and pour over chops, scraping the pan well. Bake, covered, for 45 minutes.

Sprinkle over veal:

5   ounces Parmesan cheese, grated

Preheat broiler. Return dish to oven to melt cheese just before serving. Top with chopped fresh parsley if desired.

Seafood

Fried Catfish ▪ Baked Catfish ▪ Crab Cakes ▪ Baked Fish and Cheese ▪ Fish Casserole ▪ Deep-Fried Perch Fillets ▪ Salmon Cakes ▪ Boiled Shrimp ▪ Shrimp Creole ▪ Deep-Fried Shrimp ▪ Shrimp Newburg ▪ Fried Mountain Trout ▪ Baked Mountain Trout ▪ Stuffed Flounder, Ripe Olive Sauce ▪ Genie's Tuna Surprise ▪ Shad Roe

Whether you live on ship or shore or completely inland, today beautiful fresh seafood and some beautifully frozen seafood are available at local markets. Since it is low in all those things that are bad for you and still high in the flavor department, seafood becomes more and more popular at home and in restaurants.

As with meats, the less commercial handling fish receives, the better it tastes. A whole, bone-in fish will give you more for your money than any boneless fillet you can buy. After they're cooked, most fish lose their heads quite easily and their backbones just as easily when a little expertise is applied. And the easiest way to get expertise is to do it, so try boning it yourself the next time you cook fish.

Fried Catfish

Fresh or frozen catfish can be found in almost every big grocery store in the South and is becoming popular around the country as an economical entree for your meal. Anybody can eat a pound-size catfish, most anybody can eat two, and good-sized men can put away three or more.

Fillet of catfish is certainly easier to eat, but not as flavorful as the whole fish. Bones always add flavor.

Unlike the trout, catfish is served without the head. You should buy it cleaned, skinned, and deheaded.

I would buy by head count rather than weight—three for your husband and football-playing son, maybe two for you, and one for your dieting 16-year-old daughter, and so forth.

Heat to 350° in deep fryer:

4   cups vegetable oil

Mix together in flat baking pan:

2   cups all-purpose flour
2   cups crackermeal
2   teaspoons salt
1   teaspoon freshly ground white pepper

Wash, being sure inside cavity is clean:

4   12- to 14-ounce catfish without head; 16-ounce with head

Roll fish in seasoned flour, shake off excess, and place in hot oil. Do *not* overcrowd the fryer or you will knock off some of the coating and also cool down the oil. Cook for about 20 minutes or until brown.

Serve with a slaw (page 181 or page 182), hushpuppies (page 229), French fries, sliced tomatoes, and lemon wedges.

Baked Catfish

<hr>

MAKES 4 SERVINGS

Preheat oven to 350°.

A 12- to 14-ounce catfish is usually a good individual portion. Even though you buy them cleaned and gutted, check for left-on scales. At most markets, the head on this fish has been removed; I must admit it is ugly.

Place in oiled ovenproof flat dish:

4   12- to 14-ounce catfish

Sprinkle with:

> **melted butter**
> **salt and freshly ground white pepper**
> **fresh lemon juice**
> **paprika**

Add to pan:

¼   inch water

Good options to add to help the catfish look and taste good, without changing the flavor, include:

> **½   cup white wine**
> **1   tablespoon chopped fresh parsley**
> **½   cup toasted bread crumbs**
> **½   cup sliced fresh mushrooms**

Bake, uncovered, for about 20 minutes, depending on the size of the fish. Meat should be fork-tender.

Crab Cakes

MAKES 2 SERVINGS AS AN ENTREE OR
16 SERVINGS AS AN APPETIZER

Anything with crab is good—and also expensive. See note, page xx. However, don't waste your money on cheap crab, whether "special" or not. Unless it's fresh and in good-sized pieces, another seafood will do better.

Mix:

12	ounces crabmeat (see note, page xx)
2	cups bread crumbs
2	tablespoons chopped fresh parsley
1	tablespoon grated onion
¼	teaspoon freshly ground white pepper
6	tablespoons melted butter
¼	teaspoon dry mustard
½	teaspoon Worcestershire sauce
	dash Tabasco sauce

Form into four cakes and brown in heavy frying pan in:

¼   **cup melted butter**

Try using chicken dressing (page 236) instead of the bread crumbs and leaving out the grated onion. Add a little more mustard, and you have deviled crab. Form small balls, roll in crackermeal, and fry for a change. Serve small cakes or balls as appetizers.

Baked Fish and Cheese

This time fillets do very well. Use whole fillets or cut heavy pieces into serving-size portions.

Preheat oven to 400°.

Rinse, pat dry, and sprinkle with salt and freshly ground white pepper:

> **1½ to 2 pounds white flaky fish fillets, such as cod, snapper, scamp, or whitefish**

Allow to sit a few minutes out of the refrigerator.

Combine:

> ¾   **cup melted butter**
> 3   **tablespoons chopped fresh parsley**
> 2   **tablespoons fresh lemon juice**
> 1   **tablespoon chopped fresh dill** *or* **1 teaspoon dried**
> 1   **tablespoon chopped scallion**

Place fish in buttered ovenproof pan and spoon the butter sauce over fish.

Cover dish. Bake for 35 minutes. Remove cover. Place on top of each portion:

> 1   **slice Swiss cheese**

Place under hot broiler for a couple of minutes before serving.

Fish Casserole

Preheat oven to 400°.

Combine:

⅓	cup mayonnaise (page 194)
1	10¾-ounce can cream of mushroom soup
¼	cup dry sherry
1	tablespoon fresh lemon juice

Add:

¼	teaspoon salt
½	cup chopped celery
1	scallion, chopped
1	cup sliced fresh mushrooms
1	cup cooked rice
1	cup cooked crabmeat, shrimp, scallops, or other fish or shellfish

Pour into buttered 2-quart casserole and top with:

¼	cup toasted almond slices

Bake for 15 minutes or until sauce bubbles.

Deep-Fried Perch Fillets

Heat to 350° in deep fryer:

4   **cups vegetable oil**

Mix together in small baking pan:

2   **cups all-purpose flour**
1   **teaspoon salt**
¼   **teaspoon freshly ground white pepper**

Pour into second baking pan:

2   **cups milk**

Mix in third baking pan:

1   **cup all-purpose flour**
1   **cup crackermeal**
1   **teaspoon salt**

Line up pans beside one another in order listed above.

Wash in cold water:

2   **pounds fresh perch fillets**

Dredge fillets one at a time on both sides in flour, shaking off excess, then through milk, and turn into third pan. Turn piece of fish over. Pat the flour and crackermeal well into the fish, being sure it is entirely covered with crust. Shake off excess. Place fillets on tray in a single layer. Drop carefully, one by one, into hot oil. Do not crowd the pot or put in so much that the temperature falls. Cook each fillet for 10 to 15 minutes, depending on thickness of fillets. Drain on paper towels. Serve with tartar sauce (page 217) and lemon wedges.

Salmon Cakes

Place in mixing bowl:

1   1-pound can red or good-quality pink salmon

Break salmon into flakes and mash any small bones (the bones are so
well cooked they disintegrate and add to the flavor).

Add:

1   beaten egg
½   cup uncooked chicken dressing (page 236)

Season with:

1   teaspoon melted butter
½   teaspoon salt
¼   teaspoon freshly ground white pepper
      dash Tabasco sauce
      dash Worcestershire sauce

Mix well. Divide into eight portions and pat out flat into cakes. Melt
in large frying pan:

¼   cup butter

Brown quickly for 3 minutes on each side just before serving. Top
with egg sauce (page 210) if desired.

Boiled Shrimp

Good shrimp are a beautiful pink and white color, having been graded as to size and frozen at the source of supply. If your market offers them unfrozen (unless you are in a seaside city), then almost surely the market has defrosted them.

If the shrimp have turned dark, or the shells seem hard and brittle, do not buy. Shrimp are very perishable and should be cooked within a day of being unfrozen.

Shrimp can be almost as luscious as lobster if you treat them with due respect. It is nearly impossible to undercook shrimp, but easy to overcook them. Select big shrimp, even though they cost more. You get more meat and less shell, more flavor and less preparation.

Bring to boil in 3-quart pot:

4	cups water
2	teaspoons salt
2	stalks celery, broken up (leaves add flavor)
¼	lemon, chopped, rind and all

Add to boiling mixture:

1	pound fresh shrimp in shells or frozen shrimp, defrosted under running cold water

Bring water back to rolling boil. Stir. Remove from heat. Let sit for about 2 minutes, then drain immediately by placing them in a colander which has been set in a large pot. Reserve the shrimp juice for seafood sauce (page 214). Chill shrimp quickly by running them under cold tap water. This will stop the cooking process. Drain well. Peel and devein shrimp (page 12).

Refrigerate in plastic bag with ice and 1 or 2 lemon slices sealed inside. Use within 24 hours. Serve with seafood sauce (page 214). My children love to use tartar sauce (page 217) or the salsa fresca (page 6).

Shrimp Creole

This is a mild Creole sauce flavored with shrimp, with a hint of garlic and the tang of hot sauce.

Melt in heavy Dutch oven:

    4   tablespoons butter

Add:

    1   large white onion, sliced into thin strips
    1   large green bell pepper, sliced into thin strips
    ½   rib celery, sliced thin diagonally to eliminate strings
    2   large garlic cloves, chopped fine

Sauté vegetables and garlic in butter over medium heat, 2 minutes, stirring constantly.

Add:

    2   cups shrimp stock (page 18)
    2   cups chicken stock (page 17) or canned chicken broth
    1   16-ounce can Italian tomatoes, sliced, with juice

Simmer for 10 minutes and add:

    ½   teaspoon salt
    ½   teaspoon freshly ground white pepper
    ½   teaspoon Worcestershire sauce
        dash Tabasco sauce
        pinch hot red pepper flakes (very little, very carefully—this is hot)

Mix together in separate bowl:

    2   tablespoons cornstarch
    2   tablespoons water

Add cornstarch mixture to sauce slowly, stirring well until mixture is as thick as syrup. Use more cornstarch mixture if needed. Bring back to simmer until sauce clears to a beautiful pink. Taste and reseason.

Five minutes before serving, add:

1   pound raw shrimp, 20–24 count, peeled and deveined

Simmer for 5 minutes. Do not boil. Serve over steamed rice.

Deep-Fried Shrimp

Heat to 375° in deep fryer:

> 4   **cups vegetable oil**

Mix together in small baking pan:

> 2   **cups all-purpose flour**
> 1   **teaspoon salt**
> ¼   **teaspoon freshly ground white pepper**

Pour into second baking pan:

> 2   **cups milk**

Mix in third baking pan:

> 1   **cup all-purpose flour**
> 1   **cup crackermeal**
> 1   **teaspoon salt**

Line up pans beside one another in order listed above.

Partially shell, leaving tails intact (page 12):

> 2   **pounds raw shrimp**

Butterfly the shrimp, slitting the shrimp down the outside without cutting all the way through.

Dredge shrimp one at a time on both sides first through flour, shaking off excess, then through milk, and turn into third pan. Pat the flour mix well into both sides of the shrimp, being sure it is entirely covered.

Prepare all the shrimp and place on a tray in a single layer. Carefully drop one by one into hot oil. Do not crowd the pot, cook a few at a time. Cook each shrimp for 5 to 6 minutes, until golden brown. Drain on paper towels.

Serve with tartar sauce (page 217) and lemon wedges.

Shrimp Newburg

Melt in double boiler:

> ½   cup butter

Stir in:

> 2   tablespoons all-purpose flour

Cook slowly, stirring, for 5 minutes. Do not brown.

Add slowly, stirring constantly:

> ¾   teaspoon salt
> 1   cup shrimp stock (page 18) or bottled clam juice
>   dash Tabasco sauce
> 1   cup whipping cream

Sauce will immediately begin to thicken; smoothness comes from stirring vigorously.

Add quickly while stirring:

> 1   beaten egg yolk

If mixture is too thick, thin with more shrimp stock or cream.

Add:
> 2   tablespoons dry sherry
>   salt and freshly ground pepper to taste
>   garlic salt to taste

Add just before serving:

> 1   pound raw shrimp, 20–24 count, peeled, deveined, and halved lengthwise

Simmer shrimp in sauce for 5 minutes.

Good over crisp dried toast. Garnish with chopped fresh parsley, paprika, toast crumbs, or sieved hard-boiled egg yolk.

Fried Mountain Trout

MAKES 4 SERVINGS

We get our fresh trout from Dyers & Co. in Hiawassee in the North Georgia mountains. They raise them in big cement troughs filled with cold, fast-running water. It is a very intersting place to visit, especially at feeding time.

When the trout are delivered, we clean them well, keeping the heads on, and pack them down in crushed ice; then the box is dated and placed in a very cold refrigerator. With this method, you may keep trout fresh about 48 hours. They must be packed down in ice, however, not just kept in refrigeration.

Heat to 350° in Dutch oven or deep fryer:

4 **cups vegetable oil**

Wash and check for scales not removed:

4 **fresh mountain trout**

Leave the heads on, for trout are traditionally served whole.

Mix in flat baking pan:

1 **cup all-purpose flour**
1 **cup crackermeal**
1 **teaspoon salt**
½ **teaspoon freshly ground black pepper**

Roll the trout in flour mixture, shake off excess, and place in hot oil for about 20 minutes. Coating should be beautifully browned.

Serve whole with lemon wedges and/or tartar sauce (page 217).

Baked Mountain Trout

Preheat oven to 350°.

Wash and clean:

    1   fresh mountain trout

Leave the head on, for trout are traditionally served whole.

Sprinkle trout with:

    salt and freshly ground pepper

Place in buttered baking pan.

Pour over fish from head to tail fin:

    1   tablespoon melted butter

Sprinkle with:

    paprika and chopped fresh parsley

Bake for 25 to 30 minutes. Flesh should feel firm. If it is soft, the fish is raw in the middle.

Stuffed Flounder, Ripe Olive Sauce

I don't use a microwave very much, but my brother, Paul Kennon, does well with it.

SAUCE
Melt on high in covered microwave bowl:

> 2   **tablespoons butter or margarine**

Add and mix together:

> 2   **tablespoons all-purpose flour**

Cook, covered, on high for 3 minutes, stirring each minute.

Add:

> 25   **small ripe (black) olives, pitted and chopped**
> ½   **cup olive liquid**
> ½   **cup water**

TOPPING
Place in covered microwave bowl:

> 2   **tablespoons of butter or margarine**

Melt on high for 40 seconds.

Add:

> 2   **tablespoons chopped onion**
> 2   **tablespoons chopped green bell pepper**
> 2   **tablespoons chopped celery**
> 1   **tablespoon dried parsley**

Sauté, covered, on high for 3 minutes.

Add:

> 3 slices white bread, toasted and crumbled
> 2 teaspoons hot sauce
> ½ cup water

Mix to consistency of paste.

Add:

> 1 4-ounce can tiny shrimp, drained

Combine well.

FISH
Rinse and pat dry:

> 4 4-ounce flounder fillets

Spread topping on each and roll up from wide end. Place in loosely covered buttered microwave dish. Bake on high for 9 minutes, spoon sauce over, and bake for another 3 minutes.

Genie's Tuna Surprise

MAKES 4 SERVINGS

My last child, Genie, is a "health nut." She also likes food, all kinds, and wants nothing to do with anything which is not delicious as well as healthy.

Boil or microwave until cooked:

4   medium-sized red potatoes

Steam:

2   cups freshly cut broccoli
1   cup fresh green peas

Peel and section:

1   large ripe tomato

Drain:

2   6½-ounce cans white tuna packed in spring water

Mix with:

2   tablespoons diet blue cheese or ranch dressing

Add all other ingredients and mix together lightly. Season to taste with sprinkles of curry, dill, pepper, or dried onion.

Enjoy—without guilt!

Shad Roe

Fresh shad roe is hard to find; it is in season only for two months in the springtime. You can find good-quality canned shad roe in gourmet stores and some supermarkets. Be careful when handling shad or any other fish roe, because it is very delicate, the eggs being held together only by a thin membrane. Prepare fresh or canned shad roe in the same manner.

Preheat oven to 350°.

Place in buttered flat baking dish:

   1   **whole shad roe**

Cover the roe with:

   2   **strips raw bacon**

Bake for about 20 to 30 minutes. Bacon and roe should both be done. Serve with lemon wedges.

Vegetables, Rice, and Relishes

Fresh Green Beans • Fresh Shelled Butter Beans, Lady Peas, or Field Peas • Black-eyed Peas • Hoppin' John • Baked Beans • Broccoli Soufflé • Deep-Fried Broccoli or Cauliflower • Broccoli and Cauliflower • Steamed Cabbage • Sweet and Sour Red Cabbage • Buttered Carrots • Glazed Carrots • Ginger Carrots • Creamed Celery and Almonds • Collards • Stewed Fresh Corn • Corn Pudding • Eggplant and Tomatoes • Eggplant Italiano • Eggplant Soufflé • Deep-Fried Eggplant • Baked Grits Soufflé • Mushrooms • Mushrooms Oriental • Stewed Okra and Tomatoes • Buttered Okra • Deep-Fried Okra • Steamed Okra with Black-eyes • Deep-Fried Onion Rings • Vidalia Onions • Honey Baked Onions • Deep-Fried Potatoes, New or Old • Boiled New Potatoes • Oven-Fried Potatoes • Lyonnaise Potatoes • Scalloped Potatoes • Potatoes with Cheese • Whipped Potatoes • Baked Sweet Potatoes • Sweet Potato Soufflé • Candied Yams • Pan-Fried Sweet Potatoes • Steamed Rice • Mushroom Rice • Creole Rice • Steamed and Buttered Spinach • Spinach Sautéed with Onion • Spinach Soufflé • Yellow Squash Soufflé • Deep-Fried Squash • Lyonnaise Squash • Acorn or Butternut Squash Soufflé • Baked Acorn or Butternut Squash • Scalloped Tomatoes with Onions • Fried Green Tomatoes • Stewed Tomatoes • Fresh Turnip Greens • White Turnips with Turnip Greens • Rutabagas • Chinese Stir-Fried Vegetables • Baked Macaroni and Cheese • Pickled Beets • Pickled Squash and Onions • Brandied Peaches • Green Tomato Chowchow • Green Pepper Vinegar

Vegetables are my favorite food, and I love to try new recipes. But I always come back to these simple ways, southern ways, of cooking vegetables. Sure it's fun to add herbs to the potatoes, toasted almonds and lemon slices to the rice, or a hundred thousand other variations, but these recipes are basic, and your own taste can do the rest.

My husband used to explain to customers, "God made the vegetables and not from an exact pattern. Sometimes He put more sugar in the sweet potatoes and sometimes more strings on the beans. We do our best with what He gives us."

Fresh Green Beans

We prefer pole beans to string beans because they have better flavor and fewer strings.

Snap off ends and pull off strings along sides of beans as much as possible from:

1½ pounds young tender pole beans

Break or cut into 1- to 1½-inch pieces. Rinse.

Place in heavy 1-quart saucepan:

2 **cups chicken stock (page 17) or canned chicken broth**
1 **tablespoon chicken fat or bacon drippings**
1 **teaspoon salt**
½ **teaspoon freshly ground white pepper**

Bring to a boil and add the beans. Cover and simmer slowly for 45 minutes to 1 hour.

Taste for tenderness. Drain and serve.

For a variation, add 4 to 8 small new potatoes, with or without skins, the last 30 minutes of cooking. Or slice a Vidalia onion into the beans for the last 10 minutes of cooking.

Fresh Shelled Butter Beans, Lady Peas, or Field Peas

MAKES 6 TO 8 SERVINGS

Fresh butter beans are very small, fingernail size, and are green—green pods—green beans. They're a spring vegetable here where they are raised— I've never seen them fresh (only frozen or canned) in winter. There is also a variety known as speckled butter beans, which are also small with dark red specks on them.

I see in the stores that some companies call their frozen product "small green limas."

Lady peas are small greenish white peas from a long tan pod like black-eyes.

Field peas are sisters to black-eyed peas—a little smaller.

There are, of course, dozens of different varieties of peas and beans.

Pick over and rinse:

    4   cups fresh peas or beans

Boil 10 minutes in heavy covered saucepan:

    4   cups water
    2   ounces fatback (salt pork), sliced thin

Add the fresh peas and:

    2   teaspoons salt

Simmer, tightly covered, for about 20 to 30 minutes. Add water if pan begins to boil dry. The delicate flavor does not need heavy seasoning. Serve with steamed rice, stewed corn, sliced vine-ripened tomatoes, or chopped Vidalia onions sprinkled on top.

Black-eyed Peas

Black-eyed peas are a southern food staple. The taste is unlike any other peas, for these are really beans.

Pick over:

1   **pound dried black-eyed peas**

Remove peas with spots or broken places. Rinse well through at least two changes of water.

Place in 3-quart saucepan:

4   **cups water**
¼   **pound fatback (salt pork), sliced thin, with rind removed**

Boil, covered, 30 minutes.

Add the black-eyed peas and:

1   **teaspoon salt**
1   **small garlic clove (optional)**
    more water to cover peas, if necessary

Cover tightly and simmer slowly for 45 minutes. Remove cover and check for tenderness. Remove garlic clove and discard.

If peas seem dry, add:

1   **cup chicken stock (page 17) or canned chicken broth**

Add salt to taste. Simmer until quite tender, about another 15 minutes.

Delicious served with green tomato Chowchow (page 176) and/or steamed rice (page 156) or with sliced fresh tomatoes and onions. Always serve with hot cornbread (page 230).

Note: try cooking the black-eyes with plain water. They have a nutty flavor and are good for low-fat diets.

Hoppin' John

MAKES 4 TO 5 SERVINGS

This southern dish is said to bring good luck if eaten on New Year's Day. Whether your luck is good or bad hoppin' John tastes good. I've looked in dozens of books trying to find the origin of the name with no luck at all.

Cook according to package directions:

1 **cup rice**

Prepare up to the point of removing the garlic clove:

black-eyed peas (page 120)

Add the cooked rice and:

1 **cup chicken stock (page 17) or canned chicken broth**

Simmer, covered, for 15 minutes. Add salt to taste.

Baked Beans

We don't admit these may be called "Boston Baked Beans"—unless it's Boston, Georgia.

Wash and pick over:

    2   **cups dried navy beans**

Place beans in 2-quart saucepan with:

    ½   **pound salt pork, sliced thin**
    1½ **teaspoons salt**
    6   **cups water**

Simmer, covered, for about 1 hour, until tender; most of the liquid should be absorbed. Do not drain. Preheat oven to 300°.

Mix together in long ovenproof 2-quart casserole

    2   **tablespoons chopped onion**
    2   **tablespoons brown sugar**
    1   **teaspoon prepared plain mustard**
    1   **teaspoon salt**
    ¼   **teaspoon paprika**
    2   **teaspoons vinegar**
    1   **cup catsup**

Stir in navy beans. Cover and bake for 2 hours, stirring occasionally.

Broccoli Soufflé

MAKES 4 TO 6 SERVINGS

Preheat oven to 350°.

Wash:

    2   **cups finely chopped and trimmed broccoli***

Simmer broccoli, covered, for 5 minutes in:

    1   **cup water**
    1   **teaspoon salt**

Drain and set aside.

Beat well until light and fluffy:

    4   **eggs**

Add and beat:

    2   **cups milk**
    2   **tablespoons melted butter**
    ½   **teaspoon salt**
        dash Tabasco sauce

Mix drained broccoli with egg and milk mixture and pour into buttered 2-quart baking dish. Bake for 25 to 30 minutes, until soufflé is set in the center. It should be shaky, not juicy.

---

*Frozen broccoli does very well in this recipe. Let it thaw to room temperature. There's no need to boil it; just drain well and proceed.

Deep-Fried Broccoli or Cauliflower

Prepare according to package directions:

1   cup pancake batter

Wash:

1   medium head broccoli or cauliflower

Snip off flowerets, leaving ½ inch of stem. Rinse well again and dry thoroughly.

Preheat to 350° in deep fryer:

1½ cups vegetable oil

Dip flowerets in batter and drop into hot oil a few at a time. As soon as they brown, after 2 or 3 minutes, remove to paper towels to drain. Serve immediately; they do not keep well.

Broccoli and Cauliflower

The flavors of these two vegetables complement each other well, and the colorful flowerets of both make an attractive dish when served together.

Wash:

    1   medium head broccoli or cauliflower *or*
        ½ head each

Snip off flowerets, leaving ½ inch of stem. Rinse again and drain.

Bring to boil:

    1   cup chicken stock (page 17)
    4   tablespoons butter
    1   teaspoon salt

Add vegetables and cover. Simmer gently for 5 to 8 minutes. Check for tenderness. Do not overcook.

For a variation, pour over drained flowerets:

    1   cup cheese sauce (page 203)

Serve immediately.

Steamed Cabbage

Cabbage is really a mild, delightful green vegetable as long as it is treated well. We treat it well, and our patrons love it.

Discard any yellow outer leaves, cut into quarters, and remove center core from:

1   2-pound head green cabbage

Slice or chop into bite-size pieces. Rinse under running water.

Place in heavy saucepan:

1   cup water
1   teaspoon salt
½   cup butter

Bring to simmer; add cabbage, cover, and simmer 8 minutes. Remove cover and check for tenderness. Do not overcook—cabbage should be slightly crisp. The cooking broth should be served; it makes almost as good pot likker as turnip greens.

Sprinkle cooked cabbage with:

½   teaspoon freshly ground white pepper

Add salt to taste.

Tomatoes in any fashion are a good accompaniment to the cabbage.

Sweet and Sour Red Cabbage

MAKES 6 SERVINGS

Trim off outer leaves from:

1   1½- to 2-pound head red cabbage

Cut in half, remove core, turn onto cutting board, and shred into ⅛-inch-wide strips.

Place in heavy Dutch oven:

1   cup water
1   cup apple cider vinegar
4   tablespoons white sugar
1   teaspoon salt
½   cup butter

Bring to boil. Add red cabbage and cover. Simmer for about 30 minutes. Taste.

We like to add:

⅛   teaspoon ground cloves
1   5-ounce can sliced apples*

Mix together. Simmer for another 5 or 10 minutes.

---

*Two fresh, peeled and cored sliced apples can also be cooked with cabbage for 30 minutes.

Buttered Carrots

Slim baby carrots are best, scraped lightly and cooked whole. Large carrots are also good if scraped and then cut into rounds.

Scrape (cut if necessary) and rinse:

> 1½ **pounds carrots**

Bring to a boil:

> 1 **cup water**
> ½ **teaspoon salt**
> 4 **tablespoons butter**

Add carrots and cook, covered, for 15 minutes. Check for tenderness. Drain.

Garnish with:

> 1 **teaspoon chopped fresh parsley**

Also delicious with either a sprinkle of ground ginger or ½ cup hot cream.

Glazed Carrots

Prepare:

buttered carrots (page 128)

Drain cooked carrots and return to pot.

To make light glaze, boil in separate saucepan for 2 minutes:

½   **cup water**
¼   **cup sugar**

Mix in separate small bowl:

2   **teaspoons cornstarch**
2   **teaspoons water**

Stir cornstarch mixture into glaze quickly. Simmer until clear and thickened. Add glaze to carrots. Heat through before serving.

Ginger Carrots

Scrape and cut into ¼-inch-thick rounds:

1 to 1½ pounds carrots

Simmer in salted water until tender, about 10 minutes. Drain.

Mix together in saucepan:

1	**teaspoon ground ginger**
½	**teaspoon salt**
½	**cup orange juice**
1	**teaspoon cornstarch**
2	**tablespoons butter**

Cook over low heat, stirring constantly, until thick and clear. Pour over carrots and bring back to boil.

Creamed Celery and Almonds

An unusual and excellent combination.

Cut bottom from:

> 1   **bunch celery**

Discard bottom or save to use in making soups or stocks. Snip off most of top leaves. Grasp whole bunch of celery firmly and cut on the bias into ¼-inch slices. This cutting angle eliminates most strings. Wash cut celery through two or three changes of water.

Make:

> 1   **cup cream sauce (page 207)**

Toast under broiler:

> ¼   **cup sliced almonds**

Place in heavy 1-quart pan:

> 2   **cups water**
> ½   **teaspoon salt**

Bring water to boil, add celery, and boil for 8 to 10 minutes. When celery is barely soft, drain water off and add hot cream sauce and almonds.

This also makes a nice dish without the cream sauce. Just drain celery well, toss with 2 tablespoons of melted butter, and add almonds and a sprinkle of chopped fresh parsley.

Collards

Collard greens have a stronger flavor than turnip greens and are less popular, but they are mighty good. Two pounds of these greens will usually serve four people. Always have cracklin' bread (page 230) or little fried hoecakes (page 232) to serve with them—and be sure to have on the table a bottle of green pepper vinegar (page 177).

Wash and pick over:

2   **pounds collard greens**

Discard yellow and insect-bitten leaves. Wash through several changes of water until no residue of sand or dirt is left in the bottom of the sink. Chop or shred into strips ½ by 2 or 3 inches.

Boil for 10 minutes in heavy covered pot:

4   **cups water**
¼   **pound fatback (salt pork), sliced thin with rind removed**

Add collard greens and:

1   **teaspoon salt**
1   **teaspoon sugar**

Simmer gently, covered, for 45 minutes. Test for tenderness. These greens should be almost as soft as spinach, but not quite. If pan begins to boil dry, add:

½   **cup chicken stock (page 17)**

If greens are too strong for your taste, try seasoning with:

¼   **teaspoon freshly ground white pepper**
½   **cup chicken stock (page 17)**
    dash Tabasco sauce

Stewed Fresh Corn

This is the single most popular vegetable Mary Mac's offers. We sell 300 to 500 orders daily.

Shuck:

> 5   ears young, well-filled-out white corn

Remove the silks carefully with a soft brush so as not to break open the grains. Rinse. With a very sharp knife, slice off one third of the grain all around the cob, then another third. Cut the last third off close to the cob, then scrape the remaining corn milk into a bowl.

Place corn and milk in heavy 12-inch frying pan, rinsing out the bowl with a little water to get all the corn milk.

If the corn was dry, add:

> ½ to 1 cup milk

Add to the frying pan:

> ½   cup butter or bacon drippings
> 1   teaspoon salt
> ⅛   teaspoon freshly ground white pepper

Heat, cover, and simmer slowly for 10 minutes. Check for tenderness.

Ideally this dish should thicken itself to the consistency of a heavy cream sauce. However, today's corn is different from Grandmother's, and sometimes a bit of cornstarch is indicated.

If so, mixed together in bowl:

> 1   teaspoon cornstarch
> 1   teaspoon cold milk

Add cornstarch mixture to corn while stirring. Simmer for another 5 minutes to kill the cornstarch taste. Be careful—this burns easily.

Corn Pudding

MAKES 6 SERVINGS

Cook:

>   stewed fresh corn (page 133)

Preheat oven to 350°.

Beat well:

>   2   eggs

Add:

>   1   cup milk
>   ½   teaspoon salt
>   ¼   teaspoon freshly ground white pepper
>   1   tablespoon melted butter

Mix with corn. Pour into buttered 2-quart baking dish. At this point, you may add:

>   2   tablespoons chopped onion and/or bell pepper, sautéed in butter

Bake for about 30 minutes, until slightly browned and a fork comes out clean.

Eggplant and Tomatoes

MAKES 4 TO 6 SERVINGS

Preheat oven to 350°.

Peel and cut into 1-inch cubes:

    1   **medium eggplant**
    1   **small white onion**

Boil 5 minutes in:

    2   **cups water**
    1   **teaspoon salt**

Drain eggplant and onions and add:

    1   **16-ounce can tomatoes, chopped with juice, hard cores removed**
    4   **tablespoons melted butter**
    ½   **teaspoon celery salt**
    ½   **teaspoon onion salt**
    ½   **teaspoon freshly ground white pepper**
    ½   **teaspoon dried basil** *or* **1 tablespoon fresh (optional)**

Pour into 2-quart buttered baking dish and top with:

    ½   **cup dry bread crumbs**

Bake for about 30 minutes.

Eggplant Italiano

This southern Italian dish is my favorite of all the good things my daughter Judy fixes. I don't fix it because it's so much trouble, but I sure love to eat it.

Have on hand:

    2   cups spaghetti or marinara sauce

Peel and cut into rounds ¼ inch thick:

    1   large eggplant

Salt these rounds on both sides and place in colander 30 minutes. Then rinse well, drain, and dry.

Place in separate bowls:

    1   cup Italian seasoned bread crumbs
    2   eggs, beaten lightly

Dip eggplant rounds in bread crumbs, then in egg, then in bread crumbs again. Place on baking sheet and refrigerate for 30 minutes.

Heat in skillet:

    ⅛   inch olive oil

Fry eggplant on both sides until golden brown. Drain on paper towels.

Prepare:

    1   pound mozzarella cheese, grated
    ½   cup Parmesan cheese, grated
    1   teaspoon dried basil

Butter a shallow rectangular baking dish. Preheat oven to 350°.

Layer in this order:

⅓ spaghetti or marinara sauce
    eggplant
½ mozzarella cheese
⅓ spaghetti sauce
½ Parmesan and ½ basil
    eggplant
½ mozzarella
⅓ spaghetti sauce
½ Parmesan and basil

Bake for 30 minutes. Let sit for 5 to 10 minutes before cutting into squares to serve. Wonderful!

Eggplant Soufflé

Preheat oven to 350°.

Bring to boil in heavy saucepan:

2	cups water
1	teaspoon salt

Add:

1	medium eggplant, peeled and cut into 1-inch cubes

Simmer, covered, for 10 minutes. Drain and mash. You should have about 1½ cups of pulp.

Cut crusts off:

1	slice white bread

Soak bread for one minute in:

¾	cup milk

Add:

2	eggs, beaten
1	tablespoon grated white onion
1	tablespoon finely chopped green bell pepper
2	tablespoons melted butter
1	teaspoon salt
1	teaspoon fresh lemon juice
½	teaspoon freshly ground white pepper

Add eggplant, mix well, and pour into buttered 2-quart baking dish.

Top with:

> ½   **cup dry bread crumbs**

Bake 30 to 45 minutes on the middle rack—until soufflé seems set in the middle.

Deep-Fried Eggplant

MAKES 4 SERVINGS

Combine in bowl:

> 1   **cup all-purpose flour**
> 1   **teaspoon salt**
> ¼   **teaspoon freshly ground pepper**

Roll immediately in seasoned flour:

> 1   **medium eggplant, peeled and sliced into finger-size strips**

Stir together in separate bowl:

> 1   **egg, beaten**
> 2   **tablespoons water**
> ½   **teaspoon salt**

Heat to 350° in 2-quart deep fryer:

> 4   **cups vegetable oil**

Dip eggplant in egg mix, and then in seasoned flour, shaking off excess. Fry eggplant in small batches in hot oil until golden, about 2 minutes. Keep batches warm in 350° oven until all are done. Drain on paper towels and serve immediately while crisp. Eggplant gets limp and bitter-tasting very quickly, so this should be prepared just before serving.

Baked Grits Soufflé

MAKES 4 TO 6 SERVINGS

There has been a lot of fun-making about the South's love for grits—but try this for a late Sunday breakfast or as a side dish for supper, and your guests will lap it up.

Boil:

5 cups water

Add:

1 teaspoon salt
1 cup regular grits*

Cook slowly for 25 minutes. Preheat oven to 350°.

Add to grits:

¾ pound shredded Cheddar cheese
1 cup cream
3 whole eggs, beaten until light yellow
1 grind black pepper

Bake in buttered 2-quart casserole for 25 minutes. To reheat, slice when cold and brown quickly in butter.

Mushrooms

Mushrooms cook so easily and taste so wonderful, with so few calories,

---

*Pine Mountain speckled grits are mighty good.

that they must be the world's most versatile vegetable. Appetizer, soup, salad, vegetable—I'm sure there must be mushroom desserts too.

Rinse the mushrooms lightly, then dry on paper towels. Slice them raw over a green salad; pour hot bacon drippings over them on spinach leaves; slice and pour them over a steak three minutes before taking the steak off the fire; drop into beef or pork roasts just before finishing off; add raw or cooked to gravy and of course to many sauces; add to most any soup.

Mushrooms Oriental

Mix together and bring to boil:

- ½ cup soy sauce
- ½ cup Burgundy
- 1 garlic clove, minced
- 1 tablespoon butter

Add:

- 12 ounces fresh mushrooms, any large ones cut in half
- ½ pound bean sprouts
- 1 cup chopped scallion

Simmer, covered, for 4 minutes. Add salt and freshly ground white pepper very sparingly.

Add:

- ½ cup sliced water chestnuts, drained

Heat through. Drain to serve.

For pickled mushrooms, marinate above ingredients together, but do not cook. Refrigerate overnight and serve cold. Goes well with any meat.

Stewed Okra and Tomatoes

Sometimes I think the addition of tomatoes improves any recipe. The combination of tart tomatoes and mellow okra (or eggplant) is a tastepleaser and a traditional dish to serve with peas or beans.

Place in heavy 1-quart saucepan:

1 **16-ounce can tomatoes, crushed, with juice**

Add:

1 **teaspoon salt**
1 **tablespoon sugar**
½ **teaspoon freshly ground white pepper**
2 **tablespoons butter or strained bacon drippings**

Simmer, covered, for 10 minutes.

Wash, trim, and slice into ¼-inch pieces:

½ **pound okra**

Add to tomatoes and simmer for another 5 minutes. By this time, both tomatoes and okra should be done.

If stew is still too juicy, mix together:

2 **teaspoons cornstarch**
2 **teaspoons water**

Add cornstarch mixture to stew, taste, and reseason if necessary.

Buttered Okra

Most southerners love to serve okra with black-eyed peas and an onion dish (honey baked onions, page 148, go well). Serve ham or fried chicken, black-eyed peas, and onions, and you have a southern feast!

One pound of okra should serve four to six people well, unless they are very enthusiastic okraphiles. Pick the small, tender pods. In all cases, trim the stem ends closely and rinse off well.

Bring to boil:

   2   **cups water**
   ¾   **teaspoon salt**

Add:

   1   **pound whole okra**

Boil, covered, for 10 to 15 minutes, until pods are barely soft. Drain.

Add:

   2   **tablespoons butter**

Serve immediately.

Deep-Fried Okra

Wash, trim, and slice into ¼-inch pieces:

1   **pound okra**

Prepare buttermilk wash:

½   **egg, beaten**
1   **tablespoon water**
1   **cup buttermilk**

Prepare seasoned flour mix:

1   **cup all-purpose flour**
1   **cup crackermeal**
1   **teaspoon salt**
½   **teaspoon freshly ground white pepper**

Heat to 350° in deep fryer:

2   **cups vegetable oil**

Put okra slices into buttermilk wash. Lift okra out with slotted spoon and drain well. Place in seasoned flour and shake. (My husband invented a "shaking pan" with a perforated bottom which we use at Mary Mac's, but it's not for sale!) Take out and place on cake rack and knock off excess flour. Drop in batches into hot oil until golden brown, about 2 to 3 minutes. Serve immediately.

Steamed Okra with Black-eyes

MAKES 4 TO 6 SERVINGS

In this recipe the black-eyed peas and the okra complement each other perfectly. The textures contrast and the flavors blend. All you need is a juicy slice of onion, lots of steaming hot rice, and buttered corn on the cob. Southern vegetable heaven!

Begin preparing:

black-eyed peas (page 120)

Wash, trim, and set aside:

1 **pound whole small okra pods**

During the last 15 minutes of cooking the black-eyed peas, add the okra right on top of the peas. When done, remove the okra to its own dish.

Add to the okra:

1 **tablespoon butter**

Serve the black-eyed peas and okra in separate bowls.

Deep-Fried Onion Rings

Serve these little gems with any meat or fish you wish or eat them as a snack.

Heat to 375° in deep fryer:

   4   **cups vegetable oil**

Mix together in small baking pan:

   1½   **cups all-purpose flour**
   ¾   **teaspoon salt**
   ⅛   **teaspoon freshly ground white pepper**

Pour into second baking pan:

   2   **cups milk**

Mix in third baking pan:

   ½   **cup all-purpose flour**
   ½   **cup crackermeal**
   ½   **teaspoon salt**

Line up the pans beside one another in the order listed above.

Trim and cut into ½-inch slices:

   2   **large sweet white onions**

Separate the onion into rings.

Dredge onion rings one at a time through first pan, then through the milk, and turn into the third pan. When dredging through meal mixture, be sure the onion is completely covered with meal.

Shake off excess flour. Prepare all onion pieces and place on tray. Drop one by one into hot oil very carefully. Do not crowd the pot.

Cook each for 3 to 4 minutes, until golden brown. Drain on paper towels and serve.

Vidalia Onions

MAKES 4 TO 5 SERVINGS

Vidalia onions are Georgia's award-winning sweet onions. When they are in season, we always use Vidalia onions at Mary Mac's. They are named after the town in middle Georgia where they are grown and are so sweet and crisp some folks eat them like an apple. They are good any way you fix them, even plain and simple.

Peel and slice:

2 medium Vidalia onions

Place in bowl with:

¾ cup apple cider vinegar
salt and freshly ground pepper to taste

Let soak for 30 minutes. Serve as side dish at room temperature or chilled.

Honey Baked Onions

MAKES 8 SERVINGS

Preheat oven to 325°.

Peel and trim:

4 large sweet white onions

Cut in half and place in buttered baking dish, cut sides up.

Mix in separate bowl:

1½ cups tomato juice
1½ cups water
2 tablespoons melted butter
6 teaspoons honey

Pour sauce over onions. Bake 1 hour or until soft.

Deep-Fried Potatoes, New or Old

Plan on one large potato, preferably Idahos,* per person, which will give you 16 fries if you cut the potato into four slices and then into four strips each.

These are never wasted, first because people eat them so enthusiastically and second because they make wonderful leftovers. They do well with the skin on or off, sliced as small as a pencil or as big as your finger. You can coat them with seasoned flour for crusty French fries or pat them very dry for crisp ones. Just be sure they have no bad spots and scrub them well or peel them.

---

*Sweet potatoes are wonderful as fries but must be peeled. They will turn dark if you prepare them very far ahead, so peel them, slice them, and put them in water. Before you fry them they must be patted dry.

This is a good time to use up any leftover frying oil, which I hope you have kept in the refrigerator. The potatoes will clear the oil and still taste good.

Heat to 350° in deep fryer:

4   cups vegetable oil

Freshly prepared potatoes should cook in 4 or 5 minutes. Leftovers will usually balloon up, very crisp, but need to be eaten right away before they get soggy, again. Leftovers can be kept in the refrigerator for 2 or 3 days.

Boiled New Potatoes

Allow about three small potatoes for each person. Peel them if you must, but the skin is very tender and good.

Bring to boil in heavy 2-quart pot:

4   cups water
2   teaspoons salt

Add potatoes to water. If water does not cover all the potatoes, add more. Boil for about 10 minutes, until fork-tender. Pour off water.

Add:

butter to taste
salt and freshly ground black pepper to taste

Shake to distribute the salt and butter. Serve in warm dish garnished with chopped fresh parsley.

If you have any leftovers of these, try deep-frying the next day or sautéing them in garlic butter.

Oven-Fried Potatoes

Preheat oven to 400°.

Peel long white Idahoes, 1 per person unless you are feeding teenagers—then 1½ each.

Slice ⅛ inch thick. Arrange slices on greased cookie sheet not touching. Brush with oil and sprinkle with salt and freshly ground pepper.

Cook for 15 to 20 minutes, then turn them over, brush with oil, sprinkle with salt and freshly ground pepper, and cook for another 15 minutes.

Lyonnaise Potatoes

MAKES 6 TO 8 SERVINGS

Preheat oven to 350°.

Place in large bowl:

    3   pounds potatoes, peeled and sliced ¼ to ½ inch thick
    1   large sweet white onion, chopped

Add and mix in well:

    ½   cup butter, melted
    1   teaspoon freshly ground white pepper
    2   teaspoons salt
    2   cups water

Pour into greased 2-quart baking pan. Bake for 30 to 40 minutes, until tender. Taste and reseason.

Scalloped Potatoes

Preheat oven to 350°.

Place in overlapping rows, like shingles, in oblong baking dish which can be used as a server:

    3   pounds potatoes, peeled and sliced ¼ to ½ inch thick

Place between the potatoes:

    ½   cup cold butter, sliced thin

Add:

    1   cup water
    1   teaspoon salt
    ½   teaspoon freshly ground white pepper

Bake for 20 to 30 minutes. Remove and fork-test to see if done. Liquid should be about gone.

Add:

    ½   cup warmed light cream

Reheat in oven for 5 minutes. Sprinkle with paprika and chopped fresh parsley.

Potatoes with Cheese

MAKES 6 TO 8 SERVINGS

Preheat oven to 350°.

Bake:

scalloped potatoes (page 151)

Remove the baking dish and check potatoes for doneness.

Grate:

½ **pound Cheddar cheese**

Sprinkle cheese over potatoes. Return, uncovered, to oven and bake for about 5 to 8 minutes. When cheese is melted, the dish is ready to serve.

Whipped Potatoes

MAKES 6 TO 8 SERVINGS

In this day of instant everything, real whipped potatoes are a treat.

Bring to boil in heavy 2-quart pot:

4 **cups water**
1 **teaspoon salt**

Add:

3 to 4 pounds potatoes, peeled and cubed

Reduce heat to low boil and cover. In 15 minutes, test with fork. If tender, pour off excess water or save for soup. Cover again until ready to whip the potatoes.

Pour the hot potatoes into mixer bowl and whip on low speed until all lumps are gone. Do *not* use a food processor. It will turn your wonderful potatoes to paste!

Add:

½   cup butter, at room temperature
½   to 1 cup hot milk (or cream if you want them very rich)
½   teaspoon freshly ground white pepper

The amount of milk you use depends on how thick you like your potatoes. Taste. Reseason.

If you have leftovers (unlikely), reheat in buttered ovenproof dish, perhaps with cheese sprinkled over the top.

Baked Sweet Potatoes

MAKES 6 SERVINGS

We call them sweet potatoes, Yankees call them yams. By either name, I love to eat them. Sweet potatoes are delicious—and smell so good. The Indians used to bake them in campfire ashes along with fresh corn left in the husk. Imagine those wonderful odors wafting out among the pine trees!

Preheat oven to 400°.

6   ½-pound sweet potatoes, each about the same shape, rinsed and dried

Grease with shortening and place in baking pan on aluminum foil:

Bake for 40 to 50 minutes, until completely soft. Serve immediately, slit down the middle with a pat of butter melting in the slit.

Sweet Potato Soufflé

This is one of our most popular dishes and is almost a dessert. It's a Southern tradition, especially during holidays.

Cover with water in large pot:

> **2 pounds small sweet potatoes, washed**

Boil, covered, for about 1 hour, until soft. Drain, slip skins off, and mash in large bowl. Preheat oven to 350°.

Add:

> **4 tablespoons butter**
> **4 to 5 tablespoons sugar, to taste**
> **⅓ cup light cream**
> **2 eggs, beaten**
> **pinch ground cinnamon and/or ground allspice**

This recipe involves much tasting. The sugar content of sweet potatoes varies according to season and where they are grown, so your taste must decide how much sugar to add. Pour into buttered 2-quart baking dish and bake until center of soufflé is set, 30 to 40 minutes. Raise oven temperature to 475°.

Place on top to cover:

> **miniature marshmallows**

Return to oven for 3 to 5 minutes to brown.

This recipe is also wonderful with ½ cup raisins or ½ cup toasted pecans folded in. This makes the soufflé so rich I would leave out the spice and the marshmallows.

Candied Yams

A particularly good vegetable with poultry.

Cover with water in heavy 2-quart pot:

2   **pounds small sweet potatoes, rinsed**

Boil, covered, for 20 to 30 minutes, until potatoes can easily be peeled and sliced. Drain potatoes.

Slice into ½-inch rounds and layer slices like shingles in buttered long 2-quart baking dish. Preheat oven to 350°.

Melt in small saucepan:

4   **tablespoons butter**
½   **cup brown sugar**
¼   **cup water**
⅛   **teaspoon salt**

Simmer this glaze for 2 or 3 minutes and then pour over the sweet potato slices.

Dot with:

1   **tablespoon butter**

Bake for about 30 minutes or until heated thoroughly.

Adding grated lemon rind or ground cinnamon or allspice to the glaze gives it a different taste. A teaspoon of vanilla flavoring or rum is also good.

Pan-Fried Sweet Potatoes

MAKES 6 SERVINGS

Prepare:

baked sweet potatoes (page 153)

Peel potatoes after they are baked and cut into ½-inch round slices.

Melt in heavy frying pan:

4   tablespoons butter

Quickly brown slices on both sides. Turn out onto warm platter. Scrape the pan, placing the burned butter and potato specks on the sweet potatoes to add to the flavor.

Steamed Rice

MAKES 4 SERVINGS

When I was a little girl, my mother took me to visit relatives in Batesburg, South Carolina. We stayed with aunts and cousins at several different homes, and to this day I remember each hostess going into the kitchen, getting out the rice, and then saying, "Now, what else shall we have?"

Wash in colander until water runs clear:

1   cup regular uncooked rice

Pour rice into top of double boiler and add:

1½ cups water
1½ teaspoons salt
½   tablespoon butter

Let the water in the bottom of the double boiler boil 1 hour. Top must be tightly covered. Rice should be fluffy and white.

The variations are numerous—add toasted pecans, very thin lemon slices, almonds, thinly slivered red and yellow peppers, chopped scallion.

Mushroom Rice

MAKES 4 SERVINGS

Melt in heavy skillet:

    4   tablespoons butter

Add:

    8   ounces mushrooms, caps sliced and stems chopped

Sauté 2 minutes and add:

    2   cups beef stock (page 16)
    1   tablespoon chopped onion
         dash Tabasco sauce
  ½   cup dry sherry
    1   cup raw rice

Cover and cook slowly for 20 minutes. By then, rice should have absorbed the liquid and be done.

Creole Rice

Try mixing our Creole sauce (page 208) with cooked rice to make a spicy accompaniment to pork, veal, or beef.

Steamed and Buttered Spinach

MAKES 4 SERVINGS

Remove stems and pick over:

2   pounds crisp, curly spinach leaves*

Wash through at least three changes of water, until no sand is left in bottom of sink.

Bring to boil in heavy pot:

½   cup water
1   teaspoon salt

Place washed spinach leaves in pot and cover tightly. Steam until wilted—6 to 10 minutes at the most.

Drain and add:

4   tablespoons butter

Mix and chop. Serve immediately.

---

*Much of the frozen spinach nowadays is almost equal in taste and appearance to fresh spinach. Be sure to thaw spinach overnight in the refrigerator so it will cook quickly and evenly.

Spinach Sautéed with Onion

Remove stems and pick over:

2   **pounds crisp, curly spinach leaves***

Wash through at least three changes of water, until no sand is left in bottom of sink.

Melt in large heavy frying pan:

4   **tablespoons butter**

Cook in butter for 3 minutes:

½   **cup finely chopped white onion**

Add the fresh, wet spinach leaves and:

1   **teaspoon salt**

Cover tightly and steam for 6 to 10 minutes. Chop spinach, toss lightly with the butter and onion, and serve.

---

*Frozen leaf spinach does well here, thawed, and steamed over the onions. However, pay no attention to instructions to cook it frozen. Let it thaw in the refrigerator 24 hours, then cook it.

Spinach Soufflé

Remove stems and pick over:

   2   **pounds crisp, curly spinach leaves***

Wash through at least three changes of water, until no sand is left in bottom of sink.

Bring to boil in heavy pot:

   ½   **cup water**
   1   **teaspoon salt**

Lift wet spinach leaves into pot and cover tightly. Steam for only 3 minutes, drain, and chop. Drain once again. Preheat oven to 350°.

Mix together in separate bowl:

   6   **eggs, beaten**
   3   **cups milk**
   1   **teaspoon salt**
   ½   **cup melted butter**

Add the wilted, chopped spinach. Pour into buttered 2-quart baking dish. Bake until soufflé is set in the middle, about 30 minutes.

---

*See note, page 159. Do not precook frozen spinach for this recipe, however.

Yellow Squash Soufflé

MAKES 6 TO 8 SERVINGS

This soufflé is a favorite dish throughout the South.

Bring to boil in 2-quart saucepan:

    ½   **cup water**
    ¼   **cup melted butter**
    1   **teaspoon salt**

Add:

    2   **pounds yellow summer squash, sliced**

Cook, covered, for 15 minutes. Mash in the pan with a potato masher. You should have about 1½ cups of pulp. Preheat oven to 350°.

Beat well in large mixing bowl:

    2   **eggs**

Add the squash and:

    1   **cup milk**
    1   **teaspoon salt**
    ½   **teaspoon freshly ground white pepper**
    1   **tablespoon melted butter or strained bacon drippings**

Mix well. Taste and reseason. Pour into buttered 2-quart baking dish.

Top with:

    ½   **cup bread crumbs or Saltine cracker crumbs (rolled with rolling pin until fine)**
    ½   **cup grated Cheddar cheese (optional)**

Cheddar cheese makes a good topping but can take away from the mild squash flavor. Bake for 40 to 50 minutes, until middle of soufflé is set.

Deep-Fried Squash

Prepare buttermilk wash:

- ½   egg, beaten
- 1   tablespoon water
- 1   cup buttermilk
- 1   teaspoon salt

Prepare seasoned flour mix:

- 1   cup all-purpose flour
- 1   cup crackermeal
- 1   teaspoon salt
- ½   teaspoon freshly ground white pepper

Heat to 350° in deep fryer:

- 3   cups vegetable oil

Soak in buttermilk for 5 minutes:

- 2   pounds yellow squash, sliced ⅛ inch thick

Lift out with slotted spoon and drain well. Dredge through flour mix, shake off excess, and drop into fat. Cook until golden brown, about 2 to 3 minutes. Serve immediately.

Lyonnaise Squash

MAKES 4 SERVINGS

Melt in heavy 12-inch frying pan, without browning:

- ½   cup butter

Add:

>   2   pounds small yellow summer squash, sliced
>   1   cup chopped white onion
>   1   teaspoon salt
>   ½   teaspoon freshly ground white pepper

Cover and steam slowly for 30 minutes, stirring often. Mash in the pan with a potato masher.

Add:

>   1 to 2 tablespoons light cream

Simmer for 2 minutes. Add salt and freshly ground pepper to taste.

Acorn or Butternut Squash Soufflé

MAKES 6 TO 8 SERVINGS

Either acorn or butternut squash can be used for this soufflé. The flavor is very close to that of sweet potatoes, being just a little milder.

Rinse and cut open:

>   2 to 3 pounds acorn or butternut squash

Remove seeds and boil until soft in lightly salted water. Scoop soft pulp out of shells and discard shells. Preheat oven to 350°.

Mash pulp with:

>   ¼   cup butter *or* margarine
>   ½   cup sugar
>   1   cup milk or light cream
>   2   eggs, beaten

Taste for sweetness. Pour into buttered 2-quart baking dish. Sprinkle with ground cinnamon or ground allspice if you like. Bake for 40 to 50 minutes, until the middle of the soufflé is set.

Baked Acorn or Butternut Squash

Preheat oven to 350°.

Wash well:

> **2 acorn squash *or* 1 large butternut squash**

Cut the acorn squash in half. Cut the butternut squash in half lengthwise, then take each half and cut it in half again. Remove all seeds and place squash cut side down in buttered baking pan, fairly close together.

Add:

> **water to reach halfway up squash**

Bake for 20 minutes. Remove pan from oven and pour out any water.

Turn squash cut side up and add to each piece:

> **pinch salt**
> **1 teaspoon brown sugar, sprinkled evenly**
> **1 tablespoon melted butter**

Return squash to oven and bake until meat is quite soft, about another 20 to 30 minutes, depending on size.

Scalloped Tomatoes with Onions

Melt in 10-inch frying pan:

   4   tablespoons margarine

Sauté:

   ½   cup chopped onion
   1   green bell pepper, chopped (optional)

Add:

   1   12-ounce can tomatoes, mashed, with juice
   1   teaspoon salt
   ¼   teaspoon freshly ground white pepper
   1   tablespoon sugar
   1   tablespoon strained bacon drippings
   1   cup bread crumbs (made from 2 slices day-old bread, crusts removed, torn into ½-inch pieces)

Mix all together. Add salt to taste. Pour into buttered 2-quart baking dish. Preheat oven to 350°.

Top with:

   ½   cup toasted bread crumbs*
   ¼   cup grated Cheddar cheese (optional)

Bake for 30 minutes.

---

*To make toasted bread crumbs, crush stale bread with a rolling pin into fine crumbs. Toast bread crumbs on cookie sheet in 400° oven until golden brown.

Fried Green Tomatoes

These are great, either deep-fried or pan-fried, for breakfast or with egg dishes. Allow ½ tomato (2 slices) for each person.

Rinse, trim, and cut into ¼-inch slices:

    3   **firm green tomatoes**

Beat in bowl:

    1   **egg**

Add:

    2   **tablespoons milk**
    ½   **teaspoon salt**
    ¼   **teaspoon freshly ground white or black pepper**

Mix together in second bowl:

    1   **cup all-purpose flour**
    ¼   **cup cracker crumbs**
    ½   **teaspoon salt**

To deep-fry, heat to 350° in deep fryer:

    2   **cups vegetable oil**

Turn tomato slices over in the egg mixture, then in the flour mixture, and cook gently in hot oil for 3 to 4 minutes. Drain excess fat on paper towels.

To pan-fry, heat to 350° in heavy frying pan:

    1   **cup vegetable oil**

Brown coated tomatoes on both sides. Drain excess fat on paper towels.

Some people spoon cream gravy over these slices; they're good plain or with gravy.

Stewed Tomatoes

MAKES 4 SERVINGS

Stewed tomatoes are a year-round side dish. Very good with steamed cabbage, green beans, or black-eyed peas and all kinds of meats, poultry, and fish. The trick is to get this tart vegetable to taste sweet without becoming tomato preserves.

Place in heavy saucepan:

1   **16-ounce can good-quality tomatoes, mashed, with juice, hard cores removed**

Add:

2   **tablespoons sugar**
1   **teaspoon salt**
⅛   **teaspoon freshly ground white pepper**
1   **tablespoon butter or strained bacon drippings**

Simmer, covered, for about 15 minutes.

If thickening is necessary, mix together:

1   **tablespoon cornstarch**
1   **tablespoon water**

Add cornstarch mixture to tomatoes.

Note: Either fresh basil or fresh fennel, chopped fine and sautéed in butter, does well in this dish. Of course all it takes then is some minced garlic to make this into a southern Italian dish.

Fresh Turnip Greens

A longtime favorite southern green vegetable, leafier and slightly more bitter than collards.

Wash and pick over:

3   **pounds crisp turnip greens**

Remove heavy stems. Watch out for insects, which love turnip greens too. Wash through three or four changes of water, until last water is clear and free of sand.

Bring to boil in heavy pot:

4   **cups water**
2   **teaspoons salt**
1   **teaspoon freshly ground white pepper**
¼   **pound fatback (salt pork), sliced thin**

Add washed greens, stirring them down as they wilt. Cover. Simmer briskly for about 1 hour. Remove greens, chop, and return to saucepan.

At this point the greens may be cooled and stored in their liquor in the refrigerator until you plan to serve them.

If serving immediately, bring pot of greens back to boil.

Add:

1   **cup chicken stock (page 17)**

Simmer, covered, for 30 minutes. Taste and correct seasonings. If greens are unusually bitter, add 1 tablespoon of melted chicken fat, saved from top of chicken stock, or try a very small amount of sugar. A dash of Tabasco sauce also adds zest.

White Turnips with Turnip Greens

Combine the turnips and the greens for this recipe and don't forget a sprinkle of green pepper vinegar (page 177) just before eating.

Peel, dice, and place in bowl with salted water to cover:

    1   pound white turnips

Begin preparing:

    fresh turnip greens (page 168)

About 30 minutes before greens are done, lift diced turnips from water and place on top of greens. Cover. Let steam until turnips are soft. Serve with pepper vinegar.

Rutabagas

Rutabagas are a delicious yellow turnip.

Place in 2-quart saucepan:

2   **medium rutabagas**
4   **cups water**
1   **teaspoon salt**

Cover and boil for 20 to 30 minutes. Remove cover and test for tenderness. Pour off excess water.

Add:

½   **cup butter**

Mash with potato masher.

Add:

½   **cup light cream**

Sprinkle with salt and freshly ground white pepper to taste. Mash again, taste and reseason, and reheat.

Chinese Stir-Fried Vegetables

Southern Chinese, of course.

Melt in 10-inch frying pan:

    4   **tablespoons butter**

Sauté in butter for 5 minutes:

    2   **ribs celery, sliced ⅛ inch thick**
    1   **small onion, sliced ⅛ inch thick**
    2   **scallions, sliced ⅛ inch thick, including tops**
    2   **carrots, scraped and sliced ⅛ inch thick**
    1   **small garlic clove, sliced**
    ½   **cup fresh mushrooms**
    ½   **cup sliced water chestnuts**
    ¼   **pound snow peas**
    ¼   **pound bean sprouts**
    1   **cup broccoli flowerets**

Add while stirring:

    1   **cup chicken stock (page 17)**
    1   **tablespoon soy sauce**
    1   **teaspoon salt**
    ¼   **teaspoon freshly ground white pepper**

Baked Macaroni and Cheese

Bring to boil:

6   cups water
1   teaspoon salt

Add:

4   ounces macaroni

Stir well. Simmer for 10 minutes.

Pour into colander and rinse until water runs clear. Drain almost dry. Preheat oven to 350°.

Beat until light yellow:

2   eggs

Add:

2   cups milk
½   teaspoon freshly ground white pepper
1½   teaspoons melted butter
½   teaspoon salt
2   dashes Tabasco sauce

Grate, not too fine:

1   cup Cheddar cheese

In buttered ovenproof baking dish, layer cooked macaroni, above mixture, then cheese, ending with cheese on top.

Bake for about 20 to 30 minutes, until custard is set.

You may also use as the middle layer:

1   pound ground chuck
½   cup chopped onion
1   teaspoon salt

Sauté and drain on paper towels.

Mushrooms add more taste to this casserole, and using two different kinds of cheese makes a different taste. I like the combination of Cheddar and Jack cheese, but there are infinite choices.

Relishes

Pickled Beets

MAKES 4 TO 6 SERVINGS

Mix together:

½ cup sugar
1½ teaspoons mustard seed
¼ tablespoon celery seed
1½ teaspoons salt
1 cup apple cider vinegar

Bring mixture to boil and pour over:

1 16-ounce jar sliced beets, drained

Let cool and refrigerate.

To use fresh beets, wash and cut off leaves, but do not trim root.

Place in pot of salted water to cover:

1 pound whole beets

Bring to boil, cover, reduce heat, and cook until tender, about 45 minutes to 1 hour, depending on size and age of beets. Drain, cool, peel, and slice. Pour pickling mixture over beets. Cool and refrigerate.

Pickled Squash and Onions

MAKES 6 CUPS

Scrub and slice very thin:

2 pounds small yellow squash
1 large white onion (about ½ pound)

Place one layer of squash, then one layer of onions, in flat crockery or glass baking dish.

Sprinkle with:

3 tablespoons salt

Cover with crushed ice and let stand for about 3 hours or place, covered, overnight in the refrigerator.

Mix together in 2-quart saucepan:

3 cups apple cider vinegar
4½ cups sugar
1½ teaspoons celery seed
2 tablespoons plus 1½ teaspoons mustard seed
¾ teaspoon turmeric

Bring vinegar mixture to a boil. Drain water from squash and onions. Add them to the boiling vinegar and bring mixture back to a rolling boil for 2 minutes. Cool quickly by immersing pot in sink of cold water. Place in clean glass jars with good seals and refrigerate. Will keep for about 2 weeks.

Brandied Peaches

This sauce will work with either small fresh peaches or canned peach halves. You will need a clean quart jar with a tight lid.

Place in a heavy saucepan:

> 1 cup water and 1 cup sugar *or* juice from canned
> peaches (about ½ cup)
> 12 whole cloves

Simmer for at least 5 minutes if you use the syrup, 10 minutes for the sugar water. Add:

> 1 29-ounce can peach halves *or* 1 quart small whole
> peeled peaches

Bring back to boil. Cook small peaches until soft; canned peach halves need only be heated through. Place fruit in clean glass jar.

Add to juice:

> 1 tablespoon fresh lemon juice
> ½ cup brandy

Pour over hot fruit and cap tightly. Cool and refrigerate for 1 week before using—if you can wait! This will keep for a month or more. Brandy is a good preservative.

Green Tomato Chowchow

MAKES 1 GALLON

Chowchow is so much trouble to make, it is not worthwhile to make a little—the recipe could be cut in half (we make 5 gallons weekly) to make 2 quarts, but one pint is a wonderful gift. Make your friends happy by giving them some of this special southern relish.

Grind* together:

1	small hot red pepper, washed and trimmed
4	cups washed and cored green tomato
4	cups washed and seeded green bell pepper
4	cups washed and seeded red bell pepper
4	cups chopped white onion
4	cups trimmed and chopped green cabbage

Bring to boil in heavy 2-gallon pot:

4	cups apple cider vinegar
1¾	cups sugar
4	tablespoons salt
1	tablespoon celery seed
1	tablespoon mustard seed

Add the vegetables to the vinegar mix. Boil for 10 minutes. Cool quickly by immersing pot in sink of cold water.

This makes about 1 gallon of chowchow, and it must be refrigerated. It keeps one week well and spoils after two weeks, even refrigerated. We've tried canning it, but it doesn't taste the same. Good with vegetables, especially black-eyed peas, and with beef.

---

*I use a Cleveland grinder. You may do this in a food processor by pulsing carefully—you don't want mush!

Green Pepper Vinegar

It always amazes me that this sauce is not distributed more widely in grocery stores. People come to Mary Mac's and want to buy the little bottle of pepper vinegar right off the table. In Atlanta, it is available in most stores but is easily made at home—if you can find tabasco peppers. These of course are native to Louisiana, home of Tabasco sauce, but are also grown as pot plants—very decorative with pretty little green and red peppers on a small bush. Each pepper is ½ to 1½ inches long, ¼ inch in diameter. Do not use jalapeños.

My head hostess, Edna Tippin, prepares this vinegar as gifts. It's wonderful on any kind of cooked greens; try it sprinkled on smoked oysters or clams.

Cut off stems close to:

1   cup green tabasco peppers

Rinse and set aside. (Wash your hands well after handling the peppers—these are hot.)

Carefully wash 2 cruets or stoppered small bottles. Rinse with very hot water, pack with peppers, and set in pan of hot water (to keep glass from breaking).

Bring to boil:

1   cup white vinegar

Pour boiling vinegar over the peppers. If you need more to fill the cruets, just boil more and add.

Stopper bottles and let sit for about three days before using. This does not need refrigeration and will keep for years. The peppers will last for a refilling of vinegar later on, unless some brave soul eats the peppers as well as the vinegar.

Salads and Dressings

Merle's Avocado Salad · Daddy's Slaw · Another Slaw · Chicken Salad · Nutty Crab Salad · Ginger Pear Salad · Oriental Salad · Three-Cheese Pasta Salad · Spinach Salad · Potato Salad · New Potato Salad · Vegetable Salad · Boiled Dressing · Celery Seed or Poppy Seed Dressing · French Dressing with Garlic · Mayonnaise · "Imitation" Homemade Mayonnaise · Blue Cheese Dressing · Genie's Healthful Dressing · Curry Mayonnaise · Thousand Island Dressing

Salad is a term rather like soup—almost anything goes. I prefer a cold, crisp salad, but hot potato salad is certainly delicious, and so are many molded ones. I don't know why a green salad with meat and cheese should be called a "chef's salad," but whatever you call it, it's a good meal in itself. Main dish or side dish, salads are wonderful.

Merle's Avocado Salad

There are very few gelatin salads I take the time to make, but this is a good one—pretty, fairly simple, and flavorful. My sister Merle claims not to be a cook, but she can usually be persuaded to make this for family parties.

Over 1 cup of warm (not hot) water, sprinkle:

    2   envelopes plain gelatin

Stir until dissolved.

Add:

    1   teaspoon salt
    ½   teaspoon garlic powder
    ½   teaspoon Tabasco sauce
    ¼   cup finely minced white onion

Mash:

    4   ripe avocados, peeled and pitted

Add:

    juice of 1 lemon or lime (about 2 tablespoons)

Beat gelatin mixture with wire whisk, adding avocado mixture slowly. Taste and add salt and Tabasco if necessary.

Pour into 5-cup mold and chill.

Serve on greens with homemade mayonnaise (page 194).

Daddy's Slaw

Lots of memories with this. Daddy had to make it, or it wasn't right at all. The black pepper had to be ground right over the bowl; the vinegar could be only Heinz apple cider.

Cut 1 head of hard green cabbage in half; remove core. Place cut side down on wooden board and slice very thin.

Rub salad bowl heavily with crushed garlic cloves.

Separate cabbage into strands into bowl. Sprinkle with salt and freshly ground black pepper.

Add equal amounts first of Heinz Apple Cider Vinegar, then of mayonnaise (page 194), until all cabbage is moistened or coated.

Serve with fried fish to tableful of hungry children.

Another Slaw

MAKES 7 TO 8 SERVINGS

DRESSING
Prepare:

> **4 cups mayonnaise (page 194)**

Mix together in separate bowl:

> **1 cup sugar**
> **1 tablespoon salt**
> **1½ teaspoons freshly ground white pepper**
> **4 tablespoons celery seed**
> **4 tablespoons prepared mustard**
> **1 cup apple cider vinegar**

Add to mayonnaise slowly, stirring well. Refrigerate dressing until ready to make slaw. Will keep for 2 weeks.

SLAW
Trim outer leaves from:

> **1 hard young head green cabbage**

Cut cabbage in half and remove core. Place flat side down on chopping board. With very sharp knife, shred the cabbage, cutting down into very thin slices; or use grater or cut in food processor.

Cut in half:

> **1 garlic clove**

Rub salad bowl with cut side of the garlic clove. Add cut cabbage. Pour small amount of slaw dressing over cabbage and mix well. Chill before serving.

Chicken Salad

The toasted pecans make the difference between this and "ordinary" chicken salad.

Boil until tender:

    1   **hen *or* 2 whole chicken breasts**

Remove meat from bones and chop to yield about 4 cups of diced meat.

In a mixing bowl, add to the chicken:

    2   **teaspoons grated onion**
    1   **cup chopped celery**
    1   **teaspoon salt**
    ⅛   **teaspoon freshly ground white pepper**
    1   **cup mayonnaise (page 194)**
    4   **hard-boiled eggs, chopped***
    ½   **cup toasted pecans**
    1   **tablespoon dry white wine, optional**

This salad keeps well in the refrigerator, for use on salad greens, on crackers, or in a sandwich. Chicken salad (or any meat salad) should be kept refrigerated in a covered dish. Two or three days is as long as I would keep it. After it has been unrefrigerated for any length of time, however (on a picnic, for instance), do not try to keep it any longer.

---

*If you hate to pick the shell off hard-boiled eggs as much as I do, try poaching the eggs, well done of course, or breaking them into a buttered heatproof dish and cooking them in the microwave.

Nutty Crab Salad

Rich and delicious.

Pick over and remove shell from:

    2   12-ounce cans refrigerated, pasteurized crabmeat

Add:

    1   cup chopped celery
    1   cup chopped Brazil nuts
    ¼   cup chili sauce
    ¾   cup mayonnaise (page 194)
    ¼   cup fresh lemon juice
        dill salt to taste *or* 1 tablespoon chopped fresh dill and ½ teaspoon salt
        pepper and Tabasco sauce to taste

Ginger Pear Salad

Crush with rolling pin:

    10   gingersnaps

Cream together:

    1   3-ounce package cream cheese
    3   tablespoons light cream
    ¼   teaspoon salt
    1   teaspoon chopped crystallized ginger

Mix the crushed gingersnaps and the cheese mixture. Scoop into:

6 to 8 canned pear halves, drained

Use as plate decoration or serve on greens as salad.

Oriental Salad

MAKES 6 ENTREE SERVINGS OR 10 SMALL SALADS

Pour into 2-quart mixing bowl:

1   **7-ounce jar Italian dressing**
     juice of 1 large lime *or* 2 small limes

Add to marinade and mix:

1   **cup raw broccoli flowerets**
3   **spring onions, chopped**
1   **pound cooked king crab or shrimp**
1   **pound cooked chicken white meat**

Marinate at least 24 hours. Drain before serving.

Serve on lettuce. Sprinkle with salted pumpkin seeds and red rice crackers; other very good additions are mandarin orange sections, bean sprouts, or snow peas.

This is almost a meal in itself. A soup and a dessert is all you need.

Three-Cheese Pasta Salad

Bring to boil:

6	cups water
1	teaspoon salt

Add:

2	cups small shell pasta
2	cups spinach fettuccine

Simmer for 10 to 15 minutes, until soft. Pour into strainer, rinse with cold water, and pat almost dry with paper towels.

Add to pasta:

1	cup grated Monterey Jack cheese
½	cup grated sharp Cheddar cheese
½	sweet red pepper, sliced thin
2	or 3 scallions, sliced thin

Mix:

½	cup heavy cream
½	cup fresh salad oil

Pour over pasta and mix. Taste and add salt and freshly ground black pepper.

Sprinkle over the top:

½	cup grated Parmesan cheese

Spinach Salad

Select crisp, curly spinach if you can find it. Most spinach in our markets now is the flat, straight variety, not nearly as good.

SALAD

Wash very carefully to remove all the rich black dirt from:

1   **pound fresh spinach**

Cut off any heavy stems. Roll up in clean kitchen towel and refrigerate at least an hour before using.

Sliced hard-boiled eggs and/or crumbled bacon make delightful additions.

Serve spinach salad dressing on the side.

DRESSING

Mix together:

½   **cup sugar**
1   **tablespoon dry mustard**
1   **tablespoon salt**
1   **teaspoon dried basil**
1   **teaspoon dried marjoram**
4   **garlic cloves, minced**

Add alternately, beating with wire whisk:

1½ **cups salad oil**
1½ **cups red wine vinegar**

This keeps well, refrigerated. It can, of course, be used for other green salads as well.

Potato Salad

MAKES 10 SERVINGS

Peel, dice, and boil:

    6   medium Idaho potatoes

Drain and add:

    1   tablespoon salt
    1½ teaspoons celery salt
    ½   teaspoon freshly ground white pepper
    ½   teaspoon freshly ground black pepper

Cool, then add:

    1   cup chopped celery
    1   cup finely chopped onion
    1   tablespoon plain yellow mustard
    3   hard-boiled eggs, sliced
    1   cup mayonnaise (page 194)

Mix, taste, and reseason.

If salad does not seem moist enough, add either 2 tablespoons of cream or more mayonnaise. You may wish to add 1 tablespoon of vinegar, or 1 teaspoon of sugar, or up to ½ cup of pickle relish, according to your taste.

If you fix this a day ahead and leave in refrigerator, it tastes even better.

New Potato Salad

Scrub well:

12 small new potatoes of about equal size

Add salted water to cover and boil about 10 minutes, until you can pierce one easily with a kitchen fork.

Drain and slice about ¼ inch thick. Discard any loose skin but leave enough for color.

Sprinkle with:

2 tablespoons dry white wine
2 tablespoons beef stock (page 16) or canned beef consommé

Mix lightly and let stand 10 to 15 minutes to absorb liquid.

Add:

2 tablespoons chopped scallion
1 tablespoon minced fresh parsley
1 tablespoon chopped fresh tarragon
2 teaspoons Dijon or similar mustard

Coat with:

about ½ cup vinaigrette or Italian dressing or ¼ cup each oil and vinegar

This salad is good chilled for a day, although I like it hot (or warm) about as well.

Vegetable Salad

Prepare:

broccoli and cauliflower (page 125)

Add to the broccoli and cauliflower any or all of the following barely cooked, crisp vegetables:

½ **cup carrot rounds**
½ **cup green peas**
2 **tablespoons slivered red or yellow bell pepper**

Mix gently and taste for seasoning. Sprinkle lightly with Italian dressing.

Salad Dressings

Boiled Dressing

MAKES 1½ CUPS

Boiled dressing is a southern favorite.

Mix together in saucepan:

3	tablespoons sugar
1	tablespoon all-purpose flour
1	teaspoon dry mustard
1	teaspoon salt

Stir in with whisk:

½	cup white vinegar
½	cup water
1	tablespoon melted butter

Beat in separate bowl:

2	eggs

Bring the sugar-vinegar mixture to a slow simmer, stirring constantly with whisk.

Spoon some of the lightly thickened mixture into the bowl of beaten eggs, beat lightly together, and then pour egg mixture slowly into the saucepan, stirring constantly. Beat well with whisk, bring to boil, and then remove from stove.

Pour dressing into heatproof glass or crockery container, cool to room temperature, cover, and refrigerate. Boiled dressing keeps for 2 weeks.

Excellent for potato salad or chicken salad in place of mayonnaise.

Celery Seed or
Poppy Seed Dressing

MAKES 2 CUPS

Easy to make, keeps well in the refrigerator, and very good for all fruit salads.

Boil together for 2 minutes:

½	cup apple cider vinegar
1	tablespoon white Karo syrup
⅓	cup sugar
1	teaspoon dry mustard
½	teaspoon salt
1	tablespoon paprika

Cool. Beat in slowly with whisk or in blender:

1⅓ cups vegetable oil

Add:

1	tablespoon poppy or celery seed

Chill in tightly capped bottle. It will keep a month or more. Also good on spinach salad.

French Dressing with Garlic

Beat slowly in mixer:

- ½   cup prepared mustard
- 1   cup sugar
- 2   teaspoons salt
- 2   cups tomato puree

Add alternately, a little at a time:

- 2   cups vegetable oil
- 2   cups wine vinegar

Continue to beat for 5 minutes. Stir in:

- ½   cup chopped white onion
- 2   large garlic cloves, chopped

Let sit for 30 minutes or place, covered, overnight in the refrigerator. Strain before serving with salad. The dressing will keep for approximately 2 weeks in the refrigerator.

Mayonnaise

Grandmother's best.

Beat in electric mixer, food processor, or blender:

2 eggs

Add:

1 teaspoon prepared mustard
2 teaspoons salt
¼ teaspoon freshly ground pepper
½ teaspoon paprika
1 teaspoon sugar (optional)

Add alternately and very gradually, beginning with the lemon juice:

3 tablespoons fresh lemon juice
2 cups vegetable oil

Refrigerate. Keeps for about 1 week. Wonderful with sliced tomatoes, salads, and also a good base for blue cheese dressing (page 195) and thousand island dressing (page 197).

"Imitation" Homemade Mayonnaise

When you don't have time for homemade boiled dressing or mayonnaise, squeeze the juice of a small lemon into bottled mayonnaise, beating it smooth with a fork. Add fresh parsley or your favorite herb for a very fine salad dressing.

Blue Cheese Dressing

MAKES 2 CUPS

Mix in bowl:

    1   cup mayonnaise (page 194)
    1   3-ounce wedge blue cheese, chopped

Add:

    ½   cup buttermilk
    ½   teaspoon freshly ground white pepper
    ½   teaspoon Worcestershire sauce
        dash Tabasco sauce

To thin dressing, add more buttermilk.

Serve on salad greens or use as raw vegetable dip. It will keep covered in refrigerator for about one week.

Genie's Healthful Dressing

MAKES 2 CUPS

Pour into bowl:

    1   cup plain yogurt

Add:

    1   cup buttermilk

Stir well and add:

    1   tablespoon chopped fresh dill

Use for any green salad.

Curry Mayonnaise

Daughter Judy feels this will almost certainly persuade a young one to eat broccoli or cauliflower.

Mix in small bowl:

2	tablespoons melted butter
¼	teaspoon minced garlic (or 1 large clove put through garlic press)
½	teaspoon curry powder

Add:

¾	cup mayonnaise (page 194)
1	tablespoon fresh lemon juice

Set bowl in pan of hot water over low heat. Simmer until sauce is warm. The sauce will curdle if put directly on heat. Will keep covered in refrigerator for about one week.

Thousand Island Dressing

MAKES 6 TO 7 CUPS

Prepare:

    4   **cups mayonnaise (page 194)**

Add and mix well:

    1   **cup chili sauce**
    1   **cup dill pickle relish**
    4   **tablespoons chopped pimiento**
    4   **tablespoons chopped green bell pepper**
    1   **tablespoon chopped chives**
    ½   **teaspoon freshly ground white pepper**
    3   **hard-boiled eggs, chopped**
        salt to taste
        dash Tabasco sauce (optional)

If mixture is too thick, thin with cream. Cover and refrigerate. Keeps for 2 weeks in refrigerator.

Serve on salads or as a raw vegetable dip.

Sauces and Gravies

Barbecue Sauce ▪ *Beef Gravy, Clear* ▪ *Beef or Pork Gravy* ▪ *Cheese Sauce* ▪ *Baked Chicken Gravy* ▪ *Chicken Pecan Gravy* ▪ *Fried Chicken Gravy* ▪ *Cream Sauce* ▪ *Cream Gravy* ▪ *Creole Sauce* ▪ *Egg Sauce* ▪ *Horseradish Sauce* ▪ *Parmesan Sauce* ▪ *Mandarin Sauce* ▪ *Seafood Sauce* ▪ *Sweet and Sour Sauce* ▪ *Tomato Sauce* ▪ *Tartar Sauce* ▪ *Wine Sauce*

Most chefs feel that the sauce makes the dish. I'm not a chef, but I feel that a sauce must certainly improve a dish, or it's useless. Don't let the tail wag the dog. A delicate flavor calls for a light sauce, if any—but robust beef ribs can stand right up to barbecue or horseradish sauce.

I'm sure your nutritionist has warned you against gravies. But that's all right—one of these days they'll find some unknown vitamin in gravy, especially when used on hot biscuits.

Barbecue Sauce

MAKES 4 TO 5 CUPS

This is a spicy treat.

Mix together in 2-quart saucepan:

1	quart catsup
¼	cup prepared mustard
6	tablespoons Worcestershire sauce
4	tablespoons vinegar
¾	cup finely chopped onion
6	tablespoons brown sugar
6	tablespoons melted butter

Add:

juice and cut-up rind of 3 lemons

Simmer slowly, stirring frequently, until onion is soft. Remove from heat. Let sit for 30 minutes. Strain. Brush on chicken or pork about 30 minutes before meat is done. Brush on more sauce just as the meat is finished. Also, the sauce can be served as a side dish. It will keep indefinitely in the refrigerator or it can be frozen.

Beef Gravy, Clear

Prepare and remove from Dutch oven to warm platter:

1   4- to 6-pound roast beef (page 69)

Strain juice left from beef and pour into heatproof 1-quart measuring cup. Add enough water to make 4 cups of liquid and return to Dutch oven.

Add to juice:

1   tablespoon Kitchen Bouquet
1   teaspoon salt
½   teaspoon freshly ground white pepper

Bring back to boil. Add salt and freshly ground pepper to taste. Serve with roast beef.

If you have leftover gravy, it may be refrigerated and used to reheat leftover roast.

Beef or Pork Gravy

This gravy can be made from either pork roast or roast beef.

Prepare and remove from pot to warm platter:

    1   **pork roast (page 89) or roast beef (page 69)**

Strain juice left from meat into heatproof 1-quart measuring cup. Add enough water to make 4 cups of liquid and return juice to pot.

Mix together in separate bowl:

    3   **tablespoons cornstarch**
    3   **tablespoons water**

Bring juice back to boil. Slowly add cornstarch mixture until thickened.

Add:

    1   **tablespoon Kitchen Bouquet**
    1   **teaspoon salt**
    ½   **teaspoon freshly ground white pepper**

Add salt and freshly ground pepper to taste.

For a variation, add ½ cup sliced fresh mushrooms and cook 5 minutes more. It will keep in refrigerator for about one week.

Cheese Sauce

Melt in top of double boiler:

> 2   **tablespoons butter**

Add while stirring:

> 2   **tablespoons all-purpose flour**

Cook slowly, stirring, for 10 minutes. Do not brown.

Add slowly, stirring constantly:

> 2   **cups cream or milk**
> 1   **cup shredded sharp Cheddar cheese**

Continue cooking in double boiler until cheese is melted.

Season with:

> ¼   **teaspoon salt (be careful; cheese is salty)**
> **freshly ground white pepper to taste**
> **dash Tabasco sauce**

Taste and reseason if desired.

A small amount of garlic salt adds a tang, freshly grated Parmesan cheese gives an excellent taste, and a little chopped fresh or dried parsley adds color.

Use over potatoes or baked fish or as a dip for crackers or chips. It will keep well chilled for two weeks.

Baked Chicken Gravy

MAKES 2 CUPS

This recipe is made from the stock of baked chicken (page 42), with additional giblet broth from boiling the giblets.

Place in Dutch oven in which the chicken was cooked:

all but ½ cup giblet broth from baked chicken (page 42)

Scrape down the sides of the Dutch oven to retain all the brown bits.

Combine in separate bowl:

½   cup reserved giblet broth, at room temperature
3   tablespoons all-purpose flour

Stir well into smooth paste and slowly add to broth in Dutch oven. Cook slowly, stirring constantly, for about 5 minutes to break down flour taste and thicken gravy.

Combine:

1   cup milk
1   cup water

Slowly add diluted milk to gravy mixture, beating constantly with whisk. If calories are a concern, use water only.

Beat until smooth. If gravy is too thick, add ½ cup of water or milk (milk especially if you like a rich, creamy gravy). Add salt and freshly ground white pepper to taste. If you like, add a dash of Tabasco sauce or black pepper or a pat of butter. Color is important; add a drop (only a drop) of yellow food coloring.

Add finely chopped giblets and serve with baked chicken. It will keep for one week.

Chicken Pecan Gravy

MAKES 3½ CUPS

Try this as a change from "regular gravy" with baked chicken. Pecans add a special touch and flavor.

Pour into 1-quart saucepan:

2	cups chicken stock (page 17) or canned chicken broth
¼	cup chopped red bell pepper
¼	cup chopped green bell pepper
1	teaspoon salt
¼	teaspoon freshly ground white pepper
½	cup chopped chives
½	cup chopped pecans
1	drop yellow food coloring (optional)

Bring to boil, stirring.

To thicken, mix together in separate bowl:

1	teaspoon cornstarch
1	teaspoon water

Stir cornstarch mixture into pecan gravy. Serve over steamed rice. It will keep for a few days.

Fried Chicken Gravy

This recipe is made from the drippings after cooking southern fried chicken.

Prepare and remove from the frying pan:

southern fried chicken (page 38)

Scrape the pan down, being sure to get all the little crumbs. Remove the crumbs to a warm platter.

Melt in the same frying pan:

2   tablespoons lard or other shortening

Add slowly, stirring constantly:

2   tablespoons all-purpose flour

Stir the flour while cooking for 10 minutes over very low heat, making a roux.

Now is the time to decide whether you want to make the gravy with water, chicken stock, or cream. The old-fashioned way is with water, letting the chicken drippings make the chicken flavor.

Stir in:

at least 2 cups liquid

The gravy should be smooth and brown. However, if cream is used, the gravy will have a light color.

Flavor the gravy as your family likes it, sprinkling in the seasonings of your choice:

206 • SAUCES AND GRAVIES

garlic salt to taste
freshly ground black pepper to taste
Tabasco sauce to taste
herbs to taste

Don't use wine or Kitchen Bouquet in this gravy. Let the chicken flavor hold its own. Add at last the chicken crumbs you have saved and pour gravy over lots of steamed rice, with fried chicken and biscuits. It will keep for one week.

Cream Sauce

MAKES 1½ CUPS

Melt in top of double boiler:

3   tablespoons butter

Add while stirring:

3   tablespoons all-purpose flour

Cook slowly, stirring, for 5 minutes. Do not brown. This cooks out the floury taste and adds to the rich, creamy flavor.

Add slowly, beating with whisk:

1½ cups light cream

Continue beating until sauce is smooth and thick. Add salt and freshly ground white pepper to taste. It will not keep.

Other seasonings may be added when serving the sauce with particular dishes:

parsley for new potatoes
horseradish for roast beef
garlic salt for fish fillets
chopped hard-boiled egg for salmon cakes
mustard for shrimp

Cream Gravy

Cream gravy is used with streak o'lean (page 91) and grits and other dishes as you like.

Prepare:

streak o'lean (page 91)

When you finish frying the last piece of streak o'lean, pour out the remaining hot fat into a heatproof measuring cup. Add enough bacon drippings or melted lard to make ¼ cup of fat and return fat to frying pan.

Add:

4   tablespoons all-purpose flour

Stir in flour and cook over very low heat for 5 to 10 minutes.

Add slowly:

2 to 3 cups light cream or milk

Stir constantly until sauce is creamy and thick. Add salt and freshly ground pepper to taste. It will keep for two days.

Creole Sauce

MAKES 4 CUPS

Our special spicy sauce.

Melt in large heavy frying pan:

    2   **tablespoons butter**

Add:

    2   **tablespoons all-purpose flour**

Simmer slowly for 5 minutes and add:

    1   **cup of beef stock (page 16), chicken stock (page 17)**
    2   **cups chopped fresh or canned tomatoes, with juice**
    1   **teaspoon salt**
    ¼   **teaspoon freshly ground white pepper**
    1   **teaspoon sugar**
    ½   **small dried red pepper**
    1   **garlic clove, minced fine**

Simmer sauce for 15 minutes.

Meanwhile, melt in frying pan:

    4   **tablespoons margarine**

Add:

    ½   **cup chopped white onion**
    ½   **cup chopped green bell pepper**
    ½   **cup chopped celery**
    ½   **cup chopped scallion tops**

Cook until soft, 10 to 15 minutes.

Add:

    ½   **cup sliced fresh mushrooms**

Simmer 2 minutes more. Do not overcook. Stir these vegetables into heated tomato sauce and serve with chicken, pork, beef, or seafood, or over bed of rice. It will keep covered and well chilled for two weeks.

Egg Sauce

Melt in top of double boiler:

    2   **tablespoons butter**

Add while stirring:

    2   **tablespoons all-purpose flour**

Cook slowly, stirring, for 5 minutes. Do not brown.

Add slowly, stirring constantly with a whisk:

    1   **cup light cream**

This should make a rich, smooth sauce.

Add:

        salt and freshly ground white pepper to taste
        Tabasco sauce to taste (optional)
    1   **hard-boiled egg, peeled and grated**

This is a mild sauce suitable for many dishes. Add 2 tablespoons of Chablis wine for use with seafood, or add blue cheese and serve as a raw vegetable dip, or add poppyseeds and 1 tablespoon of brown mustard for a delicious dip for fresh fruit. Egg sauce is also good served with chicken patties. Will not keep.

Horseradish Sauce

Melt in top of double boiler:

    2   tablespoons butter

Add while stirring:

    3   tablespoons all-purpose flour

Cook slowly, stirring, for 5 minutes. Do not brown.

Add slowly, while stirring:

    2   cups chicken stock (page 17)
    1   cup milk
    2¼ teaspoons salt
    1   tablespoon vinegar
    2   tablespoons freshly grated horseradish
    freshly ground white pepper to taste

Taste and add more horseradish if desired.

Good with boiled shrimp and roast beef. It will keep two weeks well chilled and refrigerated.

Parmesan Sauce

This sauce has many uses—on fish, veal, or chicken; on asparagus, broccoli, or cauliflower.

Melt in top of double boiler:

3   tablespoons butter

Add while stirring:

3   tablespoons all-purpose flour

Cook slowly, stirring, for 10 minutes. Do not brown.

Add slowly, stirring with whisk:

1   cup chicken stock (page 17)
1   tablespoon finely minced onion
¼   teaspoon freshly ground white pepper
½   teaspoon salt
dash of Tabasco sauce

Continue whisking until smooth.

Add gradually while stirring:

1   cup cream or milk
½   cup freshly grated Parmesan cheese
¼   cup Chablis

Cook for 5 minutes, until cheese is melted and sauce is smooth.

Chopped parsley or chives makes a pretty addition. It will keep well for two weeks.

Mandarin Sauce

Melt in heavy frying pan:

½   cup butter

Add:

2   cups thinly sliced onion
2   cups bamboo shoots or water chestnuts, drained
1   cup sliced fresh mushrooms

Cook, covered, for 5 minutes over medium heat.

Place in 2-quart saucepan:

2   cups chicken stock (page 17)
2   tablespoons soy sauce
1   teaspoon sugar
½   teaspoon salt
4   tablespoons dry sherry
¼   teaspoon freshly ground white pepper
    dash Tabasco sauce

Bring to a boil, stirring. Remove from heat.

Mix together in separate bowl:

2   tablespoons cornstarch
2   tablespoons water

Thicken sauce with cornstarch mixture. Add the cooked vegetables.
Taste and reseason if necessary. Add bean sprouts, if desired. Return
to the heat for just a few minutes.

Very good as a gravy for cubes or strips of cooked beef, pork, or
chicken. Add a few snow peas, dropped in at the last minute, if
desired. Serve over rice or fried noodles. It will keep two weeks
refrigerated, but does not freeze well.

Seafood Sauce

A hot and tangy sauce. My husband asked for it, and usually mixed his own, in every restaurant we ever visited.

Mix together in bowl:

2	cups catsup
1½	cups chili sauce
1	tablespoon Worcestershire sauce
3	tablespoons fresh lemon juice
2	tablespoons freshly grated or bottled horseradish
2	dashes Tabasco sauce

Stir well. Sprinkle with salt and freshly ground black pepper to taste; add more horseradish if desired. Serve cold.

This is the simplest of all seafood sauces. It will complement boiled shrimp or oysters on the half shell to the greatest degree. It will keep well, refrigerated, for at least a month.

Sweet and Sour Sauce

This is an adaption of the Oriental sweet and sour sauce (much better, of course). It's a dark red sauce depending more on the vegetables in it than the liquid for its flavor.

Melt in small frying pan:

>   2   tablespoons margarine

Sauté in margarine:

>   ½   cup thinly sliced green bell pepper
>   ½   cup thinly sliced white onion

Bring to boil in heavy 2-quart saucepan:

>   1   cup pineapple juice
>   1   cup dry sherry
>   ¼   cup soy sauce
>   ½   cup sugar
>   1   cup vinegar
>   ½   cup grenadine

Mix together in separate bowl:

>   1   tablespoon cornstarch
>   2   tablespoons water

Thicken pineapple juice mixture with cornstarch mixture, stirring well. Add the sautéed peppers and onions. Bring back to boil; thicken with additional cornstarch mixture if necessary.

Small cubes of canned or cooked pineapple may be added if you like.

Very good with either pork or chicken. It will keep well for one month.

Tomato Sauce

Melt in double boiler:

2   tablespoons butter

Add while stirring:

2   tablespoons all-purpose flour

Cover and cook slowly for 5 minutes. Do not brown. Stir gently.

Add slowly, stirring constantly with whisk:

½   **cup light cream**
½   **cup catsup**

Season with salt and freshly ground white pepper to taste.

Serve with fish or meat loaf. It will keep well covered in the refrigerator for one week.

Tartar Sauce

Prepare:

> 2   cups mayonnaise (page 194)

Mix together in separate bowl:

> ½   cup medium-grated white onion
> 2   cups dill pickle relish
> 2   teaspoons Tabasco sauce
> 2   teaspoons Worcestershire sauce
> 1   teaspoon freshly ground white pepper
> 1   teaspoon garlic salt

Stir this mixture into the mayonnaise.

Thin, if necessary, with:

> ½   cup cream

Refrigerate. Good served with fish or shrimp. It will keep well covered in the refrigerator for two months.

Wine Sauce

This is really why we sell so much bread pudding! Also, it's easy to make and goes well with ice creams and many other puddings.

Melt in double boiler:

1 cup butter
2 cups red wine
2½ cups brown sugar

Stir well with a whisk, and bring almost to a boil, until small bubbles appear around the edges.

Stir slowly into the wine mixture, beating all the while:

2 eggs, beaten

Continue beating as mixture thickens. When all the foam disappears, remove top part of double boiler from the heat and beat sauce hard with whisk. Sauce should be as smooth as syrup.

The sauce is best served hot, although it keeps well for about a month in the refrigerator or freezer. When reheating, you may need to add a little red wine for flavor.

Breads

Banana Bread ▪ *Bran Muffins* ▪ *Buttermilk Biscuits* ▪
Angel Biscuits ▪ *Beaten Biscuits* ▪ *Mile-High Biscuits* ▪
Sweet Potato Biscuits ▪ *Cornbread Muffins* ▪ *Corn Pones*
▪ *Hushpuppies* ▪ *Cracklin' Bread or Frying Pan Cornbread*
▪ *Hoecakes* ▪ *Onion Bread* ▪ *Pumpkin Nut Loaf* ▪
Apple Cheese Stuffing ▪ *Chicken or Pecan Dressing* ▪ *Cinnamon*
Rolls ▪ *Whole Wheat Rolls* ▪ *Yeast Rolls*

Southerners love their hot breads—cracklin' bread, buttermilk biscuits, hushpuppies, frying pan cornbread, and yummy yeast breads. We have also learned to love crusty French bread; sourdough bread, and those wonderful German breads you need a hatchet to get into—but nothing beats hot biscuits in the morning, with lots of soft butter and peach or strawberry preserves.

Most yeast doughs keep well in the refrigerator. Cover with wax paper, punch the dough down when it rises over the pan, and use it within two or three days.

Make your biscuit mix right up to the buttermilk addition, and it will keep, refrigerated, for a month or more. Take a little out and add enough buttermilk to make soft dough. You can quickly make a few biscuits, fresh each time this way, although leftover biscuits, split, buttered, and toasted, are nearly as good as freshly made. Mary Mac's makes about 2,000 rolls, 2,000 corn muffins, 2,000 bran muffins, and about 700 cinnamon rolls daily. Biscuits are made for parties and for variation from rolls some days.

Hot, freshly made breads of any kind are best when just made. Ideally, they go from oven to table, with few if any leftovers. Breads baked ahead for parties, or specifically for future use, should be removed from hot pans to cooling racks, then wrapped tightly in sealed bags to preserve as much flavor as possible. Most will hold well a few days in the refrigerator, or up to a month frozen. The loaves get a bit mushy in the middle when frozen and thawed, so I do not recommend freezing them. Small individual items freeze pretty well, although I do not think freezing ever preserves the original flavor.

Banana Bread

MAKES 3 MINI-LOAVES OR 1 REGULAR LOAF

This recipe is from daughter Barbara Lupo Trieglaff who has a restaurant in San Diego. These little loaves make a nice gift from your kitchen, and keep well for a week or so in the refrigerator.

Preheat oven to 350°.

Cream together:

½	cup margarine
1	cup sugar

Add:

2	eggs
½	cup milk
1	teaspoon vanilla
1	cup banana pulp (about 2 bananas)

Mix together:

2	cups all-purpose flour
1	teaspoon baking soda
½	teaspoon salt
½	cup chopped nuts

Add dry ingredients to banana mixture. Mix lightly until smooth. Fill each greased and floured pan three-quarters full.

Bake for 1 hour or until toothpick comes out of loaf clean. Remove to cool. It is delicious hot, however. Banana bread will not freeze well.

Bran Muffins

Preheat oven to 400°.

Beat:

    2   eggs

Add while beating:

    4   tablespoons sugar
    2   cups buttermilk
    6   tablespoons melted lard or shortening

Mix together in separate bowl:

    3   cups all-purpose flour
    2   tablespoons baking powder
    ½   teaspoon salt
    ½   teaspoon baking soda

Fold flour mixture slowly into egg mixture.

Stir in lightly:

    2   cups All Bran cereal

Do not overmix. The All Bran shreds should stay whole and crisp; do not let them become soggy. Pour into greased muffin tins and bake until raised and brown, about 20 minutes.

Remove from tins and cool on rack if you must cool them.

Buttermilk Biscuits

MAKES 20 REGULAR BISCUITS OR 40 TINY BISCUITS

These are a real southern favorite. The secret to good, light biscuits is a light hand in mixing the dough and rolling it out. Treat it tenderly, and you will have tender, flaky biscuits.

Preheat oven to 400°.

Mix together:

2	cups all-purpose flour
1½	teaspoons baking powder
1	teaspoon salt
½	teaspoon baking soda

Rub or cut into this mixture:

4	tablespoons lard or shortening

Rub gently with floured hands until flour and lard mixture is crumbly.

Add and mix lightly:

¾	cup buttermilk

Roll dough onto lightly floured board or marble slab. Roll to ¾-inch thickness. Add as little extra flour as possible. Cut dough to size biscuit desired (a floured glass rim will do) and place on heavily greased baking sheet. Bake for 12 to 15 minutes for regular size or 10 to 12 minutes for tiny biscuits.

These will keep, well covered, in the refrigerator for 1 week or more and toast well. If wrapped tightly, they can also be frozen.

Angel Biscuits

Very light and as good as any angel.

Preheat oven to 400°.

Place in large mixing bowl:

> 5   **cups all-purpose flour**

Add:

> 1   **teaspoon salt**
> 1   **teaspoon baking soda**
> ¼   **cup sugar**

Mix into flour mixture on low speed or by hand:

> 1   **cup shortening**

Dissolve in 2 tablespoons warm water

> 1   **package active dry yeast**

Add to liquid:

> 2   **cups buttermilk, at room temperature**

Pour the liquid slowly into the flour mixture, mixing steadily but lightly.

Roll out ½ inch thick on floured board. Cut into small rounds and place on greased baking sheet. Bake for 20 minutes. These are delicious with ham or sausage filling or with butter and preserves.

Beaten Biscuits

There must be a story behind this—some colonial maiden wishing for the crisp crackers of her homeland, I suppose. There is a hotel in Perry, Georgia, which is famous for these biscuits. My children asked to go by Perry every time we went to Florida, just to have them. They are a challenge to make, but wonderful for special occasions.

Preheat oven to 350°.

Mix together:

      3¾ **cups all-purpose flour**
      1   **teaspoon salt**
      ⅛   **teaspoon baking soda**

Rub in:

      ¼   **cup shortening**

Add slowly:

      1   **cup skim milk**

The dough should be very stiff. Knead it until smooth, then form it into a ball. Place ball on heavy wooden block on top of a very sturdy cabinet. Beat the ball flat with a heavy mallet; form into a ball again and repeat this procedure until the dough begins to blister, about 30 minutes. Roll out, cut into small rounds, and bake on greased baking sheet until brown, probably 30 minutes. They will be crisp and light, perfect to use with ham or sausage for little sandwiches. They store in refrigerator or freezer beautifully for one month or more. Do not store, though, after filling.

Mile-High Biscuits

These are my sister-in-law Phyllis's contribution. She says that when even she can always make a recipe succeed, it has to be good.

Preheat oven to 450°.

Sift together:

> 3   cups all-purpose flour
> 4½   teaspoons baking powder
> ¾   teaspoon cream of tartar
> ¾   teaspoon salt
> 2   tablespoons plus 1½ teaspoons sugar

Mix in:

> ¾   cup shortening

Beat:

> 1   egg

Add to:

> 1   cup milk

Add liquid mixture to flour mixture quickly and lightly. Turn out onto floured board and knead just a few times, also lightly.

Roll dough out 1 inch thick. Be sure your biscuit cutter is this deep—you can, of course, cut the dough into triangles or whatever you fancy. Place on greased baking sheet and bake for 10 to 12 minutes. The biscuits freeze well, or store in refrigerator for a day or two.

Sweet Potato Biscuits

These biscuits have the sweet taste of the sweet potato; just add a pat of butter and pop them into your mouth.

Boil in water to cover for 40 minutes or until soft:

1   large sweet potato

Drain. Let potato cool, then peel and mash with potato masher.

Beat in large mixing bowl:

2   eggs
½   cup sugar

Add 1 cup of the mashed sweet potato and mix well. Taste for sugar.

Then add and mix into dough:

2   tablespoons softened butter
3   tablespoons softened shortening
1   teaspoon salt
4   teaspoons baking powder
2   cups all-purpose flour (½ cup at a time)

Preheat oven to 350°.

Turn dough onto lightly floured board or marble slab. Flour hands and knead lightly three or four times. Roll out to ¼-inch thickness. Cut with 2-inch biscuit cutter. Place on ungreased baking sheet. Bake for 15 minutes. Sweet potato biscuits store well in the refrigerator for a day or two, in the freezer for a month.

Cornbread Muffins

Preheat oven to 500°.

Beat well:

> 3   eggs

Add and mix well:

> 3   cups buttermilk
> 2   tablespoons sugar
> 4   teaspoons salt
> 4   tablespoons melted lard or shortening

Add to mixture:

> 3   cups yellow cornmeal
> 1   cup all-purpose flour
> 2   tablespoons baking powder
> 1   teaspoon baking soda

Mix lightly; do not beat.

Measure 2 heaping tablespoons of mixture into each well-greased muffin cup, filling almost to the top. It is not necessary to heat the muffin tins first if you use a very hot oven; this will create crusty sides.

Bake the muffins for 15 to 18 minutes. Serve hot.

The muffins freeze well. To store, cool, place in plastic freezer bags, and keep in freezer (as long as you can stand it).

Corn Pones

Don't ask me where the word pone *came from—I really never thought about it until now. A pone is a portion of cornbread shaped with your hands into an oval and baked in an old black cast-iron skillet. I'm sure we will hear from a reader who has the real story of how this delicacy got its name—I'll let you know.*

Preheat oven to 450°.

Mix together:

> 1 **cup yellow cornmeal**
> ½ **teaspoon salt**

Add:

> 1 **cup boiling water**

Shape into 3 pones and place on hot greased skillet. Brush well with:

> 2 **teaspoons melted fat**

Bake for about 20 minutes.

Crisp and delicious with soup, pot likker, and vegetables. To store, cool, place in plastic freezer bags, and keep in freezer.

Hushpuppies

MAKES APPROXIMATELY 24 HUSHPUPPIES

On the riverbank, when we finished cooking and feeding all the fishermen, the dogs were howling mournfully. So we stirred up the rest of the cornmeal and buttermilk, made it into balls, and fried them in the pot in which we'd cooked the fish. We gave it just a few minutes to cool, threw it to the dogs, and they really did hush up! That is really where the name came from. And that's why catfish lovers cook hushpuppies in the same fat in which the fish are fried.

Heat to 350° in deep fryer:

> ·4   cups lard or vegetable oil

Mix together:

> 2½   cups cornmeal (yellow or white)
> ½   cup all-purpose flour
> 2   teaspoons baking powder
> 1   teaspoon salt
> 1   tablespoon sugar

Add:

> 1¼   cups buttermilk or flat beer
> ⅔   cup chopped onions (or more to taste)
> ½   cup bacon drippings or melted lard
> 1   egg, beaten

Mix together lightly. The batter should be a little stiff. Drop by the heaping teaspoon into hot fat. They should bounce to the surface in 2 or 3 minutes. Turn hushpuppies and brown for another 2 or 3 minutes. Remove hushpuppies and drain on paper towel.

For a side dish, slice onion rings, roll in dry hushpuppy mix, and deep-fry for 3 minutes. Remove and drain on paper towel.

Hushpuppies are perfect with fried catfish (page 98).

Cracklin' Bread or Frying Pan Cornbread

This recipe reminds me of frosty winter mornings when I was small. The first really cold spell was hog-killing time on the farm (no refrigeration other than the weather, of course). Part of the procedure was stripping off the fat and rendering the lard by cooking the fat in a big iron kettle over an open fire. The liquid fat was poured off and stored, and the bits of lean left in the kettle were called "cracklin's." The hams were hung in the smokehouse— other pieces were salted and stored in our coldest outdoor shed—and we had lots of fresh pork during the winter.

Cracklin' bread refers to the crispy pieces of fatback cooked in the cornbread. They add a wonderful texture and taste. Pan-frying the cornbread gives it crusty sides as well.

Preheat oven to 350°.

Mix together:

　　1½　cups white cornmeal
　　½　cup all-purpose flour
　　1　tablespoon baking powder
　　1　teaspoon salt

Beat in separate bowl until light yellow:

　　2　eggs

Add to eggs:

　　1½　cups buttermilk
　　1　tablespoon melted lard or fatback or bacon drippings

Stir in the cornmeal mixture lightly.

For cracklin' bread, chop into small cubes:

2   ounces fatback

Brown cubes in heavy 9-inch frying pan. Remove with slotted spoon to the cornbread batter. The remaining rendered drippings may be used to substitute for the above tablespoon of melted lard, the rest kept for future use in seasoning vegetables.

Pour the cornbread batter back into the hot frying pan. Bake until top is golden brown, about 30 minutes.

The cornbread is easily removed from frying pan by placing a plate over it and inverting pan. Cut into squares or triangles.

Serve with turnip greens (page 168), pot likker (page 20), and at any dinner meal.

Cracklin' bread does not store well or freeze well.

Hoecakes

These are nice little cornmeal pancakes, really good with soup or with turnip greens.

Mix together:

2	cups all-purpose white or yellow cornmeal (not self-rising)
½	teaspoon salt
1	cup hot water
2	tablespoons melted shortening or bacon drippings

Add:

1	to 1½ cups cold water (enough to make batter pour easily)

Cook on hot griddle, about 2 tablespoons for each hoecake.

Unless you have a griddle that doesn't need greasing, use enough shortening to prevent the pancakes from sticking.

The pancakes do not store or reheat well as muffins; however any leftovers can be used in making chicken dressing.

Onion Bread

MAKES ABOUT 24 PIECES

The odor from this is wonderful and will probably attract lots of visitors to your kitchen. It goes well with any kind of meat, especially broiled steaks.

Preheat oven to 450°.

Melt in large frying pan:

    ¼   **cup lard or shortening**

Add and sauté:

    2   **pounds onions, sliced**

Sprinkle over onions:

    2   **tablespoons salt**

Set aside.

Mix together:

    4   **cups all-purpose flour**
    2   **tablespoons baking powder**
    1½ **teaspoons salt**

Add:

    ¾   **cup lard**

Mix until crumbly.

Mix together:

    2   **eggs, beaten**
    2   **cups milk**

Add egg mixture to flour mixture, stirring very lightly.

Grease one 18- by 12-inch baking sheet. Spread mixture over the pan. Cover with sautéed onions.

Mix together:

    1   **egg, beaten**
    1   **cup sour cream**

Spread this over the onions. Bake for about 25 minutes.

Wrap tightly and store for a day or two in the refrigerator. It does not freeze well.

Pumpkin Nut Loaf

MAKES 1 BUNDT PAN OR 4 MINI-LOAF PANS

Daughter Barbara Trieglaff says you should measure everything into the bowl, then mix it. Nice and easy recipe, delicious pumpkin bread.

Preheat oven to 350°.

In large mixing bowl, combine:

5¼ cups all-purpose flour
4½ cups sugar
2¼ teaspoons ground cinnamon
¾ teaspoons ground nutmeg
3 teaspoons baking soda
2¼ teaspoons salt
1 cup water
6 eggs, beaten
1½ cups vegetable oil
1 cup chopped nuts
1 14-ounce can pumpkin *or* 2 cups mashed cooked fresh pumpkin

Pour into greased and floured pans. Bake for 1 hour. It keeps well in the refrigerator but does not freeze well.

Apple Cheese Stuffing

MAKES ENOUGH TO STUFF 2 CHICKENS OR 1 CHICKEN WITH A SMALL SIDE DISH.

My great-grandchildren live in Germany with their parents, and their mother, Debbie, number one granddaughter, loves to cook. She sent this recipe, which the two little boys enjoy.

Combine in bowl:

> 2½ cups toasted bread cubes
> 1⅓ cups chopped apple

Melt in small frying pan:

> ⅓ cup margarine

Sauté:

> ½ cup chopped celery
> ½ cup chopped onion
> ½ teaspoon seasoned salt

Pour the celery mixture over the bread mixture and stir well.

Sprinkle over all:

> 1½ cups freshly grated Parmesan cheese

Toss lightly.

If made as a side dish, bake at 350° for 35 to 40 minutes in a casserole.

Chicken or Pecan Dressing

Good cornbread and rolls make a great deal of difference in making chicken dressing to go with Baked Chicken (page 42). If you do not have frozen chicken stock (page 17) on hand, mix all the ingredients below except the stock and wait until you can get some broth from the hen you are baking. The dressing can be used to stuff the hen, but does well as a separate dish.

Stores in refrigerator for several days, but does not freeze well. Do not try to keep dressing which has been used as stuffing.

Prepare:

6 cornbread muffins (page 227)
3 white rolls or yeast rolls (page 240)

Beat in large mixing bowl:

3 eggs

Add and stir well:

2   cups chicken stock (page 17)
½   teaspoon freshly ground white pepper
1   teaspoon salt
½   cup chopped onion
½   cup chopped celery
¼   cup melted butter

Crumble cornbread muffins and rolls into mixture. Let mixture sit for 30 minutes. Preheat oven to 350°.

Pour mixture into 2-quart baking dish and bake for 30 minutes or until mixture sets.

For pecan dressing, add ½ cup of pecan pieces before baking mixture.

Cinnamon Rolls

MAKES 24 ROLLS

Our student customers from all the colleges nearby can't get enough of these!

Prepare:

yeast rolls dough (page 240)

After dough has risen twice, divide it into four portions for easy handling. Roll each portion onto lightly floured board or marble slab. Roll each portion of dough very thin into a long strip about 8 inches wide.

Have prepared:

½   **cup melted butter**
½   **cup sugar**
1   **teaspoon ground cinnamon**
½   **cup raisins (optional)**
½   **cup chopped pecans (optional)**
    any fruit (pineapple, peaches, cherries), drained

Preheat oven to 400°.

Brush the rolled-out dough portions with the melted butter, using a pastry brush. Sprinkle heavily with sugar and cinnamon. Also sprinkle evenly with fruits and nuts (amounts depend on how filled you like your rolls).

Carefully roll dough like jelly roll, beginning with long side, and slice in circles ¼ to ½ inch thick.

Place the cinnamon rolls on buttered baking sheet barely touching each other. Sprinkle with additional cinnamon and sugar and let rise in warm place for 15 to 20 minutes. Bake until they smell too good to wait another minute, about 30 minutes. They store well in the refrigerator for a day or two, a month in the freezer.

Whole Wheat Rolls

Preheat oven to 400°.

Melt:

> ½   cup butter

Add:

> ¼   cup sugar

Warm but do not boil:

> ⅔   cup milk

Add:

> 1½ packages active dry yeast

Beat:

> 2   eggs

In large mixing bowl, combine these 5 ingredients. Then slowly add:

> 1½ cups whole wheat flour
> 1½ cups all-purpose flour

Beat slowly for 5 minutes, turn out onto floured board, and knead until smooth.

Let rise in warm place until double, punch down, and let rise until double again.

Roll out about ½ inch thick, cut into rounds, and double over for Parker House–type rolls. Place on oiled baking sheet and let rise until double again. Brush melted butter over tops and bake for 10 or 15 minutes, until well browned. Brush again with melted butter if you wish or if they are to be reheated and used later.

These have the whole wheat flavor but are much lighter than usual. They freeze well for up to one month.

Yeast Rolls

Preheat oven to 400°.

Place in ½ cup warm (not hot) water:

1	package active dry yeast
½	teaspoon sugar

Let yeast stand 5 minutes, until it bubbles.

Mix in separate bowl:

2½	cups all-purpose flour
1	tablespoon sugar
1	teaspoon salt
3	tablespoons melted lard
1	egg, beaten
½	cup evaporated milk, undiluted and warm
3	tablespoons mashed potatoes (leftovers or made from dried flakes)

Add activated yeast to flour mixture and beat well with bread hook for at least 5 minutes. If you are not using a mixer, turn this mixture onto a marble slab or floured board and knead it for about 5 minutes or until dough is smooth and elastic. Allow dough to rise in warm place, covered with cloth and out of drafts, until double in bulk.

Punch down, cover, and let rise until again double in size, about 1 to 2 hours.

Place dough on lightly floured board or marble slab. Pinch off dough in teaspoon-size pieces and drop two in each greased muffin tin.

Cover and let rise in warm place until double in size again. Bake until brown, about 25 minutes. Remove from oven. Glaze top with melted butter.

Of course, the best thing to do with these rolls is to serve them immediately, hot and wonderful.

If this does not fit your plans, remove them from tins to cool. They store well, tightly covered, for a few days in refrigerator; they freeze well. Few flavors last more than a month in the freezer.

Desserts

Apple Cake • Apple Brown Betty • Applesauce Cake with Lemon Sauce • Applesauce • Banana Cake • Carrot Cake • Chocolate Buttermilk Cake • Dessert Puffs • Dump Cake • Fruit Cobblers • Gingerbread • Peach Crisp • Pineapple Pecan Cake • Pound Cake • Easy Brownies • Sweet Fruit Soufflés • Atlanta West's Famous Chocolate Chip Cookies • Peanut Butter Chews • Sugar Cookies • Apricot Custard • Banana Pudding • Boiled Custard • Bread Pudding • Carter Custard • Cherry Cheese Cup • Chess Pudding • Mocha Mousse • English Plum Pudding • Hard Sauce • Lemon Sauce • Rum Custard • Chocolate Fudge Sauce • Strawberry Shortcake • Pastry • Bourbon Pecan Pie • Chess Pie • Key Lime Pie • Individual Fruit Pies • Sugared Pecan Halves

Puddings are a traditional southern dessert, from light soufflés to the heavier bread pudding. This chapter is where you can be especially creative—try a different flavoring; add a bit of bourbon or liqueur; use lots of nuts. I guarantee your audience will love it.

Cakes are more trouble but worth it. We read a lot about chocoholics, but strangely enough, chocolate desserts have the fewest addicts at Mary Mac's. Banana pudding, bread pudding with wine sauce, and cherry cheesecake have their special days, and I am not allowed to plan any differently, unless I also plan to leave town that day.

Apple Cake

Use tart red apples for this recipe.

Preheat oven to 350°.

Cream together in large mixing bowl:

2	cups sugar
1	cup butter or margarine

Add and stir well:

2	eggs
2	cups all-purpose flour
1	teaspoon salt
1	teaspoon ground cinnamon
1	teaspoon ground nutmeg

Mix together in separate bowl:

2	teaspoons baking soda
4	tablespoons hot water

Add this mixture to batter.

Pare, core, and slice very thin:

5	cups tart red apples

Stir gently into batter the apples and:

1	cup walnut or pecan pieces

Pour batter into greased and floured 10-inch tube pan and bake for about 45 to 50 minutes. Test cake by inserting a toothpick; if toothpick is clean when removed, cake is done.

Cool to room temperature, invert, and remove from pan.

Apple Brown Betty

MAKES 6 TO 8 SERVINGS

Preheat oven to 350°.

Mix together:

3	cups graham cracker crumbs
1½	cups sugar
1	cup melted butter
1	cup pecan pieces

Divide mixture into two parts. In long 2-quart baking pan, spread and pat down one half of the mixture.

Pour over the graham cracker mixture:

1	16-ounce can applesauce *or* 2 cups fresh applesauce

Mix together and sprinkle over the applesauce:

½	cup sugar
1	teaspoon ground cinnamon

Carefully pat the remaining half of the graham cracker crumb mix over the applesauce. Bake for 20 to 30 minutes. Crust may not brown, but it is done when applesauce begins to bubble. Let cool for 15 to 20 minutes. Cut into squares. Remove from pan with a spatula to serving dishes.

Applesauce Cake with Lemon Sauce

MAKES 1 8-INCH SQUARE CAKE

Preheat oven to 350°.

Pour into small bowl:

    1   **cup water**

Add and soak:

    ½   **cup raisins**

Set aside.

Cream together in separate large mixing bowl:

    ½   **cup shortening**
    1   **cup sugar**

Add:

    2   **eggs**
    1   **teaspoon salt**
    ½   **teaspoon baking soda**
    ½   **teaspoon ground cloves**
    1   **teaspoon ground cinnamon**
    2   **teaspoons baking powder**
    1   **16-ounce can applesauce** *or* **2 cups fresh applesauce**

Slowly add the drained raisins and:

    2   **cups all-purpose flour**
    ½   **cup pecan pieces**

Mix well and pour into 2-quart greased and floured glass baking dish. Bake for 40 minutes.

While cake is baking, prepare lemon sauce for topping.

Boil in small saucepan:

1   cup water

In top of double boiler, stir together:

½   cup sugar
1   tablespoon cornstarch
     pinch salt

Add the cup of boiling water while stirring. Cook, stirring, for 20 to 30 minutes, until sauce is thick and clear.

Remove from heat and add:

2   tablespoons butter
2   tablespoons fresh lemon juice
     dash ground nutmeg

Stir well.

Test cake for doneness by inserting a toothpick in cake. If toothpick is clean when removed, cake is done. Cut into squares of desired size while still in baking dish and spoon lemon sauce over servings. Serve warm or cold.

Applesauce

Wash, pare, core, and slice:

8 tart red or green apples

Place in saucepan with:

water cover

Simmer until tender. Water should be absorbed. Drain off any excess. Mash with potato masher or blend until soft and pulpy.

Stir in:

½ **cup sugar**
1 **teaspoon fresh lemon juice**
⅛ **teaspoon ground cinnamon**

Cook gently for 3 minutes more.

Serve as a dessert or as a side dish with pork.

Banana Cake

MAKES 1 9-INCH CAKE

Preheat oven to 350°.

Cream until soft and fluffy:

    ½   **cup shortening**

Add:

    2   **eggs**

Beat for 5 minutes and add:

    2   **cups cake flour**
    1   **teaspoon baking soda**
    ½   **teaspoon salt**
    4   **tablespoons buttermilk**
    1   **teaspoon vanilla**
    2   **large ripe bananas, mashed**
    ½   **cup chopped pecans**

Mix well and pour into buttered and floured 9-inch cake pan. Bake until browned, about 30 minutes.

No icing is really needed—it is best eaten while hot, but does well with chocolate sauce and ice cream too.

Carrot Cake

MAKES 1 10-INCH TUBE CAKE

Preheat oven to 325°.

Beat together until very light:

4 eggs

Add and beat:

1 cup vegetable oil
1 cup honey

Mix together in separate bowl:

2 cups cake flour
2 teaspoons baking powder
½ teaspoon baking soda
½ teaspoon salt

Gradually add the flour mixture to the egg mixture, beating slowly all the time.

Add:

1 teaspoon vanilla
1 cup grated raw carrots

You may want to add 1 cup of chopped pecans here; we like the plain cake with pecans in the icing.

Pour batter into greased and floured 10-inch tube cake pan. Bake for 1 hour, until cake springs back to the touch. Cool to room temperature, invert, and remove from pan.

To make carrot cake icing, mix at low speed:

6 to 8 ounces cream cheese, at room temperature

Add slowly:

¼   cup light cream
2   cups confectioners sugar

This icing should be just right to pour over the tube cake, letting it drizzle down the sides and into the middle.

Chocolate Buttermilk Cake

MAKES 1 8-INCH CAKE

Preheat oven to 350°.

Place in saucepan:

½   cup water
2   ounces dark chocolate
½   cup butter

Bring to boil and set aside.

Place in mixing bowl:

1   cup sugar
1   cup cake flour

Add the melted chocolate and:

¼   cup buttermilk
¾   teaspoon baking soda

Stir in:

1   egg

Pour into 8-inch greased and floured pan and bake for about 30 minutes.

To make the frosting, melt:

3   tablespoons butter

Stir in:

3   tablespoons cocoa
1½ cups confectioners sugar

Beat until smooth. Add hot coffee if necessary to make the icing spread easily.

Dessert Puffs

These are fun to make and evoke many compliments. You can use almost any filling, from chicken salad to puddings or any mixture soft enough to stuff into the little puff. It's an easy recipe but calls for lots of beating.

Preheat oven to 425°.

Bring to boil in a heavy 2-quart saucepan:

    ½   **cup water**

Add:

    ¼   **cup butter**

Let butter melt, then add:

    ½   **cup all-purpose flour**
    ¼   **teaspoon salt**

Stir with wooden spoon quickly and evenly. Lower heat; beat mixture until it makes a ball and leaves the sides of the pan. Remove from heat and cool slightly, about 5 minutes.

Beating vigorously each time, add one at a time:

    2   **eggs**

Beat until mixture is smooth.

Drop by teaspoonful onto greased cookie sheet at least an inch apart. They will rise and brown quickly. Bake for about 15 minutes. Remove from oven and cool before you stuff them.

Suggestion: when cool, cut open and fill with ice cream. Freeze. Serve as needed with hot fruit or chocolate sauce.

Dump Cake

MAKES 1 9- BY 13-INCH CAKE

Daughter-in-law Babs has two little girls and a hungry husband, so she cooks a lot when she's not at the Tea Room, and she likes her recipes quick, easy, and good to eat.

Preheat oven to 350°.

Dump into greased 9- by 13-inch pan:

1   20-ounce can crushed pineapple in syrup

Spread out evenly with a rubber spatula, then dump in:

1   21-ounce can sweet cherry pie filling

Spread into an even layer and pour over it:

1   package dry yellow cake mix

Sprinkle over the cake mix:

1   cup chopped pecans
1   stick butter, cut into thin slices

Bake for 50 to 55 minutes, cut into squares, and enjoy.

Fruit Cobblers

Fresh apples, peaches, cherries, or berries are the best, of course, but good-quality canned or frozen fruit also does very well in cobblers.

Preheat oven to 350° if using fresh fruit, to 400° for canned fruit.

Prepare:

½   **recipe pastry (page 280)**

Roll pastry out to fit top of 12-inch-long by 8-inch-wide baking dish. (Thirteen by nine is okay too.)

For fresh fruit, rinse, cut out overripe spots, or peel if necessary. Fresh apples do fine with skin on, peaches should be peeled, etcetera.

2   **pounds fresh fruit**

Place fresh fruit in bowl and add:

1   **cup sugar**

For canned fruit, use:

1   **16-ounce can fruit in heavy syrup, undrained**

Canned fruit usually contains enough sugar; however, additional sugar may be added to taste.

Pour fruit into baking dish and dot with:

½   **cup butter**

Cover with pastry, crimp the edges, and cut vent holes in the top. Glaze crust with melted butter. If using fresh fruit, cook for 1 hour; if using canned fruit, cook for 25 to 30 minutes. The cobbler is done when the pastry is golden. Serve warm.

Gingerbread

Preheat oven to 350°.

Cream together:

1	cup vegetable shortening
1	cup sugar

Add and beat well, one at a time:

2	eggs

Then add:

1	cup dark Karo syrup
2½	cups all-purpose flour
1	teaspoon salt
2	teaspoons ground ginger
1	teaspoon baking soda
1	cup buttermilk

Pour into a greased 9- by 13-inch baking pan. Bake for 30 to 35 minutes.

Peach Crisp

This is a very old country recipe from down around Fort Valley. A customer sent it to me originally, and I changed it a bit. It is very quick and easy to make, a good way to use ripe fresh peaches, and children like it. Serve hot with vanilla or peach ice cream on top.

Preheat oven to 350°.

Combine:

1	cup sugar
1	cup dry biscuit mix (your own or commercial)
½	teaspoon ground cinnamon
1	egg, beaten
1	cup milk

Melt in baking dish:

1	stick butter

Pour batter into melted butter. Do not stir.

Arrange over the batter:

3	cups sliced peeled fresh peaches

Sprinkle with:

1	cup brown sugar

Bake for 35 minutes.

Pineapple Pecan Cake

MAKES 1 10-INCH TUBE CAKE

Preheat oven to 325°.

Beat until light in color and fluffy:

    3   eggs

Add and continue to beat:

    2   cups sugar
    1   cup vegetable oil

Mix together in separate bowl:

    2   cups cake flour
    1   teaspoon baking soda
    ½   teaspoon salt

Fold flour mixture slowly into egg mixture.

Add:

    1   16-ounce can crushed pineapple, undrained

Pour batter into greased and floured 10-inch tube cake pan. Bake for 50 to 60 minutes, until cake springs back to touch. Cool to room temperature, invert, and remove from pan.

To make pineapple pecan icing, melt in top of double boiler:

    1   cup butter or margarine

Add while stirring;

    1   cup sugar
    ¾   cup evaporated milk

Boil for 6 minutes.

Add and mix:

      1   **cup flaked coconut**
      1   **cup crushed pineapple, undrained**
      ½   **cup pecan pieces**

Let cool. Spread on cake.

Pound Cake

Preheat oven to 350°.

Cream:

> 2 cups butter
> 2 cups sugar

Beat in separate bowl for 1 minute:

> 6 egg yolks

Add egg yolks at once and beat.

Add gradually:

> 3 cups cake flour

Beat in separate bowl for 1 minute:

> 6 egg whites

Fold egg whites into batter.

Add:

> ½ teaspoon salt
> 2 teaspoons vanilla

Beat well. Pour batter into greased and floured 10-inch tube pan. Bake for 1½ hours, until cake springs back to touch. Cool to room temperature. Invert to remove from pan; set upright to serve.

Easy Brownies

Preheat oven to 350°.

Cream together:

1	stick butter, softened
2	cups sugar

Add:

6	eggs
1	16-ounce can chocolate syrup
3	cups all-purpose flour
1	tablespoon baking powder
¾	tablespoon vanilla

Pour into greased and floured 9- by 13-inch baking pan and sprinkle with pecans. They will sink into the batter, and you can use as few or as many as you like.

Bake for 20 to 25 minutes, until slightly browned. Cool in pan, then cut into squares.

Sweet Fruit Soufflés

This does well with peaches or apricots or any berries.

Preheat oven to 450°.

Melt:

    3   **tablespoons butter**

Stir in:

    3   **tablespoons flour**

Add slowly:

    1   **cup milk *or* part milk and part fruit juice**

Add:

    ½   **cup sugar**
         dash salt

Bring to simmer. Remove from heat. This should be very thick but smooth. Whip with a whisk if necessary.

Add:

    1   **cup fruit, drained**
    ½   **cup sugared or glazed pecans**

Add:

    4   **egg yolks, beaten**
    2   **drops almond or lemon extract**

Beat until stiff:

    4   **egg whites**

Fold them into the fruit mix very carefully.

Pour into buttered and sugared 2-quart soufflé dish. Place dish in pan. Pour in hot water till it reaches halfway up the sides. Bake for 15 minutes, turn oven down to 375°, and bake 20 to 25 minutes more.

This is delicious hot, with a sweet sauce, a liqueur sauce, or the following lemon sauce.

Atlanta West's Famous Chocolate Chip Cookies

MAKES 6 DOZEN 3-INCH COOKIES

Daughter number one, Barbara, has a restaurant in San Diego and does lots of beautiful catering. This is a cookie she's been making for years, at home and at the restaurant.

Preheat oven to 400°.

Beat:

4	eggs

Add:

2	cups soft margarine
1½	cups brown sugar
1½	cups white sugar
2	teaspoons vanilla

Mix together:

4½	cups all-purpose flour
2	teaspoons baking soda
2	teaspoons salt
1	16-ounce package chocolate chips
2	cups oatmeal

Pour wet ingredients slowly into dry ones and mix gently.

Spoon onto greased pan—teaspoon for small cookies, tablespoon for large ones. Leave lots of room for spreading.

Bake for 15 to 17 minutes, until light brown.

Will keep cookie monster satisfied at least 2 days.

Peanut Butter Chews

Another Barbara specialty.

Preheat oven to 325°.

Cream together:

⅔	cup butter
1	cup brown sugar
2	cups white sugar
1	cup peanut butter

Add:

4	eggs, beaten
2	teaspoons vanilla

Combine:

2	cups all-purpose flour
2	teaspoons baking powder
1	teaspoon salt
1½	cups rolled oats
1½	cups flaked coconut

Pour egg mixture slowly into flour mixture, stir together, and pour into greased 9- by 13-inch baking pan. Bake for about 30 minutes. Do not overcook.

For the topping, mix together:

1½	cups peanut butter
1	cup powdered sugar
2	tablespoons water

Spread this topping over the cake while it is still warm. Cut in squares in pan. Serve warm.

Sugar Cookies

Preheat oven to 400°.

Cream together:

½   **cup butter**
¾   **cup sugar**

Add:

1   **egg, beaten**

Mix well, then add in order:

1½ **cups cake flour**
½ **teaspoon baking powder**
¼ **teaspoon salt**
2   **tablespoons heavy cream**
1   **teaspoon vanilla**

Chill 1 hour.

Roll out very thin and cut into any pattern.

Place on greased cookie sheet and sprinkle with sugar. Bake for 6 minutes, until the edges brown.

Vary this recipe by adding ½ cup chopped pecans, raisins, or candied citrus peel or ½ cup crushed peppermints.

Apricot Custard

This comes from an Ansley Park neighborhood party, where Nina Collins's pudding successfully competed with many fancy desserts.

Preheat oven to 350°.

Combine:

3   **egg yolks, beaten**
3   **eggs, beaten**
1   **cup sugar**

Beat until creamy.

In saucepan, combine:

1½ **cups milk**
1   **cup heavy cream**

Bring to boil and remove from heat.

Add:

1½ **teaspoons vanilla**

Pour into egg mixture and stir thoroughly.

Butter 1½-quart baking dish.

Sprinkle into dish:

½   **cup chopped dried apricots**
½   **cup golden raisins**

Pour the egg-cream mixture over the fruit. Dust lightly with ground nutmeg.

Place baking dish in a heavy pan; pour in enough very hot water to come halfway up sides of dish. Bake until set, 45 minutes to 1 hour. Custard is more delicious warm, but is also good when served cold.

Banana Pudding

Prepare:

    6   cups boiled custard (page 269)

Have on hand:

    1   13½-ounce box vanilla wafers
    6   ripe bananas

Alternately layer 1-quart serving dish with one layer of wafers, one layer of bananas, sliced ¼ inch thick, and one layer of custard.

Cover tightly and place in refrigerator until ready to serve or for at least 1 hour. If desired top when serving with whipped cream.

Boiled Custard

Boiled custard is an old-fashioned dish that is never, never boiled. My mother used to fix it, and I ate my part hot. However, it is best to cool and refrigerate it.

Pour into top of double boiler:

4   cups milk

Let milk get hot and steamy but do not boil.

Beat in mixing bowl until light and fluffy:

4   eggs

Add to eggs and beat:

1   cup sugar

Pour 1 cup of the hot milk into egg mix and stir well. Then slowly pour this mixture back into double boiler with the rest of the milk. Stir constantly until milk barely comes to boil. The consistency should be thick enough to coat a spoon. If not, continue to cook but do not boil.

Remove from heat. Pour custard into heatproof glass dish with cover. Set aside to cool, covered, at room temperature.

When cooled, stir in:

1   teaspoon vanilla or lemon extract

Cover. Store in refrigerator. Custard spoils easily; eat as soon as possible.

Bread Pudding

Preheat oven to 350°.

Cut crusts off:

10 slices white bread

Let bread soak for 5 minutes in:

1½ cups milk

Beat in large mixing bowl until light in color:

3   eggs

Add bread, milk, and:

¾   cup sugar
1   tablespoon baking powder
3   tablespoons melted butter
**2   cups fruit such as apples, peaches, or cherries, cooked
     or fresh, sweetened and drained**

Mix together well and pour into buttered 2-quart baking dish. Bake
for 30 minutes or until pudding sets. Serve with wine sauce (page
218). Best served hot.

Carter Custard

We get political at election times and make up new desserts to suit my notions of the candidates. The Carter custard recipe has been in more cookbooks and magazines than any other recipe at Mary Mac's. We called it Jimmy Carter Custard when Mr. Carter first started running; president's pudding a month before he won the election, and Carter custard since.

Beat together:

6	ounces cream cheese, at room temperature
¾	cup milk
½	cup peanut butter
1	cup confectioners sugar

Beat until firm in separate bowl:

1	cup whipping cream

Fold cream into cheese mixture very gently.

To make pie crust, mix in bowl:

1½	cups graham cracker crumbs
¾	cup sugar
6	tablespoons melted butter

Pat crumb mixture into bottom and sides of 9-inch pie plate.

Pour the custard into the graham cracker crust.

Top with:

chopped unsalted dry-roasted peanuts to cover

Freeze the custard and then serve.

Cherry Cheese Cup

Cream together:

8	ounces cream cheese, at room temperature
2	eggs
¼	cup sugar
½	teaspoon vanilla

Divide this mixture into six individual cups.

Top with:

1	16-ounce can red pie cherries in heavy syrup
	whipped cream to cover (optional)

Chill in refrigerator.

Chess Pudding

Another old-time dessert, baked instead of cooked in a double boiler.

Preheat oven to 350°.

Beat until light in color:

4	eggs

Cream together in separate bowl:

    ⅔   **cup butter**
    1   **tablespoon all-purpose flour**
    1   **tablespoon cornmeal**
    2   **cups sugar**
    ¼   **teaspoon salt**

Add beaten eggs and:

    2   **cups milk**
        juice of 2 lemons

Pour into buttered 1-quart baking dish and bake for 40 minutes. Serve hot or cold.

Mocha Mousse

MAKES 12 SERVINGS

Cream together:

    8   **ounces cream cheese, at room temperature**
    ¾   **cup milk**

Add and mix well:

    2½   **cups chocolate fudge sauce (page 278)**
    ½   **cup coffee liqueur**

Fold in gently:

    4   **cups whipped cream made from 1 pint whipping cream (whipped until stiff enough to form peaks)**

Divide among 12 6-ounce dessert bowls.

Sprinkle with:

    sliced almonds

Cover and chill in refrigerator until set.

English Plum Pudding

MAKES 80 OUNCES, OR 5 POUNDS

This is an old recipe from Phyllis Siefferman's family. In fact, she notes that everybody in the family should be present while this pudding is being made and that each one should take part in the stirring, even if only for a minute. This ensures the good health and good luck of every family member.

Mix together:

1	pound raisins
¼	pound citron (orange, and lemon peel), chopped fine
¼	pound golden raisins
½	cup chopped almonds

Sift over the fruit and nut mix:

1	cup all-purpose flour

Mix together:

2	cups bread crumbs
½	cup sugar
1	teaspoon ground cinnamon
½	teaspoon each ground allspice and ground cloves
1	teaspoon salt
1	cup good-quality suet, chopped fine (ask your butcher)

Add:

1	cup molasses
3	eggs, beaten
1	teaspoon grated raw carrot
1	cup brandy

Add last:

the fruit and flour mix

Butter sixteen 5- to 6-ounce molds for steaming the pudding.

Fill each mold two-thirds full, cover securely, and steam for 4 hours. Few people, other than the English, have real steamers. Make a homemade one with a tightly lidded Dutch oven into which you place a cake-cooling rack to set the molds on. Add hot water and place over very low heat. Check often to be sure there is still enough hot water to steam. Or place molds in long pan with ½ inch water, seal tightly with aluminum foil and place in 350° oven. Check batter for doneness; if center of pudding is still a bit mushy, steam further. Large molds may take up to 8 hours.

Store these puddings in airtight containers and, when ready to use, steam again for about 30 minutes. Remove from mold, pour brandy over the pudding, ignite it, and carry into your slightly darkened dining room. Serve with hard sauce (page 275) or lemon sauce (page 276).

Hard Sauce

MAKES 1½ CUPS

Cream:

1   stick butter at room temperature
1   cup sugar

Add:

1   tablespoon flavoring—vanilla, rum, or lemon

The sauce will stand in stiff peaks when chilled but will melt easily over a hot dessert such as English plum pudding (page 274).

Lemon Sauce

In top of double boiler, mix:

½ cup sugar
2½ tablespoons all-purpose flour
¼ teaspoon salt

Beat separately:

2 egg yolks

Add to the egg yolks:

1 cup water

Stir into the sugar mixture. Cook, stirring, 10 minutes.

Remove from heat and add:

1 tablespoon butter
¼ cup fresh lemon juice
1 teaspoon grated lemon rind

Liqueur or brandy may be substituted for the lemon juice and rind.

Rum Custard

Mix together:

    1   cup sugar
    4   tablespoons plain gelatin
    4   tablespoons all-purpose flour
    1   teaspoon salt
    1½ cups milk powder

Beat slightly:

    4   egg yolks

Add and stir until smooth:

    1   cup cold water

Add the gelatin mixture to the egg yolk mixture and stir well. Pour into heavy saucepan and add:

    4   cups hot water

Bring to boil and simmer, stirring constantly, until thick. Set aside to cool, then add:

    2   tablespoons melted butter
    2½ tablespoons rum

Pour into six individual molds or one large one. Place in refrigerator until serving time. Serve with whipped cream if you wish or with sugar cookies.

Chocolate Fudge Sauce

MAKES 2 CUPS

In top of double boiler, melt:

6   tablespoons butter

Add:

2   cups confectioners sugar
⅔   cup cocoa
¾   cup cream

Beat until smooth. Bring to boil, stirring frequently, and cook 5 minutes. Should be very thick, especially for mousse.

Strawberry Shortcake

I've heard lots of stories about why this is called shortcake—it's a shortcut to making cake; it's a very "short" dough; and so on. Whatever the reason for its name, it is one of the most beautiful and luscious of desserts, especially in the middle of the summer. Of course we can get strawberries all year, but full summertime is the time for red, ripe, downright satisfying, sun-ripened berries.

Preheat oven to 400°.

Mix together:

2   cups all-purpose flour
1½   teaspoons baking powder
1   teaspoon salt
1   tablespoon sugar
½   teaspoon soda

Rub or cut into the mixture:

½　cup lard

Rub gently with floured hands until the flour takes up all the shortening.

Add and mix lightly:

¾　cup buttermilk

Turn out on floured board and knead a few times with base of hands. Cut with biscuit cutter or into any shape you desire. Place on greased baking sheet. Bake 10 minutes or until browned on top.

Rinse and hull:

1　pint strawberries

Slice into bowl and sprinkle with:

½　cup confectioners sugar

Leave at room temperature 10 minutes to draw juice from the berries.

Beat until it holds stiff peaks:

1　cup whipping cream

Add:

1　teaspoon confectioners sugar
1　drop vanilla extract

Split the shortcakes open, pour strawberries over bottom half and top. Add a generous dollop of whipped cream, and garnish with more strawberries.

Pastry

MAKES 4 SINGLE-CRUST PIE SHELLS
OR 2 DOUBLE-CRUST PIE SHELLS

Flaky and wonderful. This is our basic recipe for dessert pastries as well as pot pies.

Cream in mixer or by hand:

> 1 cup lard
> 1½ teaspoons salt
> 1½ teaspoons sugar

Make:

> ⅔ cup ice water (with crushed ice)

Measure:

> 3½ cups all-purpose flour

Add ½ cup of the flour slowly to lard mixture. Mix together lightly in mixer or by hand. When mixture becomes stiff, add 1 tablespoon of ice and water. Repeat process until all flour and water is used. Mixture should be soft but not wet. Refrigerate.

When ready to use pastry in pies and turnovers, roll out dough on lightly floured board or marble slab. Flour hands also when handling dough to prevent sticking.

This pastry can be kept several weeks sealed in a plastic bag in the refrigerator. It can be frozen up to one month.

Bourbon Pecan Pie

Preheat oven to 375°.

Combine in heavy saucepan:

    1   **cup dark Karo syrup**
    ¾   **cup sugar**
    ¼   **teaspoon salt**

Bring to rolling boil, stirring steadily, for 2 minutes. Remove from heat and add:

    3   **tablespoons butter**

Beat in separate bowl:

    3   **eggs**

Pour hot syrup mixture slowly into eggs, beating with wire whisk.

Add:

    1   **cup toasted pecans**
    ¼   **cup bourbon**

Pour into unbaked pie shell (page 280) and bake for 45 to 50 minutes, until filling is firm. Cool before cutting.

To make this really sinful, add ½ cup chocolate chips along with the pecans and bourbon.

Chess Pie

Making pastry is no big deal, you know—and ours (page 280) is better than the ones you buy. But everybody's time is valuable and limited, so use the frozen piecrusts you buy at the grocery if you wish.

Preheat oven to 400°.

Beat and set aside:

3 eggs

Mix together:

2 cups sugar
2 tablespoons all-purpose flour
2 tablespoons cornmeal
¼ teaspoon salt

Place in mixing bowl:

1 cup cream
1 teaspoon vanilla
½ cup melted butter

To the cream mixture, add the sugar mixture, stir well until all dry ingredients are melted, then add the beaten eggs.

Brush pie shell with butter, prick, and bake about 10 to 15 minutes before you pour the filling in. It should be turning a light tan, done enough to keep the custard from soaking in.

Pour filling into pie shell and bake for 15 minutes, until custard is set.

Key Lime Pie

A legendary pie from Florida's Key West, it graces any table and makes a dessert to look forward to. Edna Tippins, our beautiful hostess, gets many requests for this as she is expert in making it. Light, rich, and delicious.

Dissolve in 1 cup boiling water:

> 1   3 ounce package lime Jell-O

Add:

> ½   cup fresh lime juice
> 1   teaspoon grated lime rind

Beat:

> 2   egg yolks

Slowly add Jell-O mixture and:

> 1   14-ounce can Eagle Condensed Milk

Stir well and chill until thick.

Beat and fold into thickened Jell-O mix:

> 2   egg whites

Pour into graham cracker pie crust. Chill. Before serving, top with whipped cream.

Individual Fruit Pies

Prepare:

  1   **pastry recipe (page 280)**

Place in heavy 2-quart saucepan:

  1   **8-ounce package dried peaches or apples**

Add and stir together:

  2   **cups water for peaches, 4 for apples**
  ¾   **cup sugar**
  ½   **teaspoon salt**
  ½   **teaspoon ground cinnamon**
  1   **teaspoon fresh lemon juice**

Cover tightly and simmer for 20 to 25 minutes. Fruit should have absorbed all the water and be quite tender. Pour off excess, if any. Mash with potato masher or whirl in blender until mixture is smooth. Taste and reseason.

Preheat oven to 350°.

Roll out pastry on lightly floured board or marble slab and cut into eight circles, each 6 inches in diameter. Divide the fruit mixture among them. Fold pastry over in half, crimp edges together with a fork, and pierce pastry for vent holes.

Brush with melted butter and sprinkle with sugar to taste.

Place on greased baking sheet and bake for 20 to 25 minutes, until brown.

These also make wonderful fried pies. Leave off the butter and sugar on the outside of the pie pastry.

Heat to 350° in deep fryer:

4   cups vegetable oil

Gently drop individual pies into hot oil and fry for about 10 to 12 minutes, until golden brown. Drain on paper towels. Sprinkle with confectioners sugar.

Sugared Pecan Halves

MAKES 2 CUPS

Preheat oven to 250°.

Mix together in bowl:

3   tablespoons cold water
¾   cup sugar
¾   teaspoon salt
½   teaspoon ground cinnamon
2   egg whites

Pour into mixture:

1   pound (2 cups) whole pecan halves

Spread pecans out on greased cookie sheet. Bake for 1 hour. Remove to another greased cookie sheet to cool at room temperature.

Index

About the Author

I come from a long line of strong southern women, as my children sometimes bitterly remind me. My husband was a strong man also, with his own produce business. When he lost his business through a series of mishaps and we decided the time had come for him to come into Mary Mac's full-time, sometimes twenty-four hours of togetherness erupted—always at home, never in public—and the household would seek cover. And there were a lot of them *to* seek cover—for quite a few years our household consisted of my mother, his mother, my son from a previous marriage, his three daughters from a previous marriage, and our two daughters; also four dogs, two cats, a lot of tropical fish, and, of course, us two. Nevertheless, it was a good marriage, thirty years of it, with much more happiness than hassles, and I miss every minute of it. My husband died over six years ago, and I still often think, "I'll have to talk that over with Harvey."

The children were raised in the business. My son and my number five daughter are strong right arms at the Tea Room still; number one daughter has her own successful restaurant in San Diego and does a beautiful job of catering too; number two daughter teaches at nearby Georgia State and is working on her doctorate; number three is raising children at this point; number four is also busy with little ones. I have fourteen grandchildren and two great-grandchildren, so I answer to any version of "grandmother." My daughter-in-law and my sons-in-law are wonderful, and they mostly say "Yes, ma'am." They all love Mary Mac's, and so do I.

My philosophy? Do what you have to do, and enjoy it. My advice to young ones—find out what you enjoy doing most, and do it. There has to be a way of making a living that is more than looking forward to getting off at five o'clock or getting a pension after thirty years. I'll never be rich, but I sure have enjoyed my life.

I love to read cookbooks, and obviously you do too. The regional or ethnic recipes have so much history behind them, as well as so much desire to please family and friends, that it is a joy to read them and to read between the lines also. I have several friends who have written very successful cookbooks, and as I read them I can feel each one's love of people and each one's wish to feed and nourish them—the essence of southern hospitality.

I wrote this book to show any cook interested in southern cuisine, family style, exactly how to produce it. Atlanta has become such a cosmopolitan city that it has restaurants with ethnic menus from African to Asian. I am sure, though, that there will always be a place for southern food, because it's good food, and healthy food.

Southern hospitality has always been linked to southern food—to food grown in this region and cooked the same way our grandmothers and great-grandmothers cooked. While I've made sure to retain all the "goodness," I've tried to take out some of the "badness"—the fat and cholesterol—that everyone is so conscious of today, and I hope you and yours will have lots of good meals from these pages.